FROM THE
TRENCHES

FROM THE TRENCHES:

Advice to Parents Raising a Child With Special Needs

Carol L. Prosser

A Mother's Story of Survival

arbor books

FROM THE TRENCHES
Carol Prosser

1. Title 2. Author 3. Parenting & Family/Children with Special Needs

Library of Congress Control Number: 2006926318
ISBN: 0-9777764-6-8

DEDICATION

I wish to dedicate FROM THE TRENCHES to my very most favorite son and his older sister, my very most favorite daughter. My children are blessings and my greatest challenge.

Love you both loooooooooooooooooooooooooooooooooooong time,

Mom

I also wish to dedicate FROM THE TRENCHES to all parents of special needs children who preceded me in the trenches along with the parents who are currently struggling in the trenches and future parents who will do their best to survive the trenches. It is my sincere hope and prayer that you will find the necessary supports to sustain you and that you, in turn, will encourage and educate others. You can survive. You will survive. May you have angels all around you!

ACKNOWLEDGEMENTS

I wish to acknowledge the memory of my grandmother, Anna Krahn. She was a quiet, humble woman with a strong faith which she boldly shared. For this I will be *eternally* grateful.

I wish to acknowledge my junior and senior high school English teachers: Mrs. Landby, Mrs. Hallan, and Mr. Atwater. Without them I wouldn't possess the necessary skills to write nor would I have a love of writing.

Thanks to Kathy and Bonita from Trumpet Design, Inc. When FROM THE TRENCHES was ready to be published I met Kathy and Bonita. They not only supported my publishing efforts but they inspired me to include artwork produced by people with special needs. I applaud you in your efforts to seek better lives for special needs individuals and I hope that your book LITTLE KITE takes flight and soars high soon!

Thanks to Brett's artwork FROM THE TRENCHES has an amazing and unique cover design. Thanks to Brett, Jan, and Shana for sharing their artistic gifts that give FROM THE TRENCHES life and incomparable dimension.

by
Brett

TRUTHS FROM THE TRENCHES

INTRODUCTION

During the *survival* years many people told me that I should write a book. I was exhausted and far too busy back then but I always thought that others could learn from my experiences.

When I mentioned writing a book about Sam to my husband he looked at me and asked, "What's the purpose of the book?" I didn't have a ready answer.

When I told my very most favorite daughter who knows everything that I was going to write a book about Sam she said, "Good. I hope that your book goes better than my photo album," and she flashed her perfect smile at me. (The photo album she referred to was to have been ready for her high school graduation six years earlier and was still sitting in shoe boxes.)

Not to be discouraged, I got a notebook and began jotting down ideas.

Some time later I attended a women's event where the motivational speaker was an author. After listening to her I knew that I could write my book about Sam. So, I got out my notebook and began expanding on my ideas.

Frequently while I was writing I would think of my husband's question, "What's the purpose of the book?" I wanted other families in similar situations to know that they weren't alone. I wanted other families with handicapped children to know that they could and would survive but there was more.

When I read the Valentine's Day greeting card, "When you were a baby we changed you eight to ten times a day," and the inside of the card read, "Now we wouldn't change anything about you. Happy Valentine's Day, Son," I knew the purpose of my book about Sam. The real purpose of this book is to *celebrate* Sam. In a broader perspective, the purpose of this book is to celebrate all handicapped individuals.

It is my hope and prayer that others can and will learn from this book. I hope and pray that hurting families with handicapped children will learn that they can and will survive and that their handicapped children have value. It is my hope and prayer that if any periphery people like health care providers, educators, friends, or general public folks read this book that they will realize that judgment is not helpful. They can choose to be either part of the problem or part of the solution.

Most of all, I want to celebrate my very most favorite son, Sam. And, as Sam *always* says, "Mom, I am your **only** son."

ASSURANCE GIVEN

It shouldn't have happened. But, it did. It should never happen again. But, it may.

My husband and I had one beautiful and nearly perfect child and we wanted more children. Due to health issues I had been advised to wait to have more children. So we waited. While waiting we attempted to adopt children without success. Ironically, my surgeon told me to wait and have my own so that I knew what I was getting.

When Sabrina was eight years old a near and dear friend offered to keep her for the week-end so that Dick and I could celebrate our anniversary. A couple months later I realized that I was pregnant. Imagine that: thirty-four years old and pregnant. While elated at the thought of a baby I was terrified to think of the physical ramifications. I didn't know if I was up to it but I was pregnant and as they say in the circus, "The show must go on."

I soon found an obstetrician at a well respected medical facility. At my first appointment I expressed my concern about pregnancy and delivery since I have some paralysis. This young and exuberant obstetrician assured me that I had nothing to worry about because he had assisted quadriplegics deliver babies. (When I had a check up with my surgeon he assured me that this delivery would not be a piece of cake.)

Prenatal visits were uneventful although the obstetrician and I never did agree on a due date. I was thirty-four years old and I knew exactly when I conceived but I was patient with him. After all, he was a doctor. As the months passed I was getting so big and so uncomfortable and he seemed so unconcerned. When I expressed my concern he just smiled at me. For three weeks at my weekly appointment I told him that I thought that the baby was getting too big. I even suggested that there was a possibility that the radiation therapy I had years earlier could be preventing the pituitary gland from setting labor in motion. He smiled at me in his patronizing way and assured me that my baby was just fine. It just wasn't time.

The last prenatal visit was a Thursday and I was loaded for bear. I was so miserable and so concerned about the welfare of my baby. I gave the obstetrician an ultimatum: Either you get this baby out of me or I will go someplace where they will. He told me that if I didn't deliver over the week-end to come in Monday and he would induce me. The following day I delivered Sam as naturally as a nine pound fifteen ounce baby can be delivered. After delivery I never saw my obstetrician until my six week check up at the clinic at which time he never inquired about my baby. I was so thrilled with my new son and I had pictures to share but he never asked.

Sam was born with miconium aspiration pneumonia and a Group B Strep infection. The first ten days of his life were spent in NICU where we didn't know from day to day if he would live or die or if he would be blind or deaf. It all seemed like a nightmare and I just prayed that I would take my baby home. I was so focused on taking Sam home that it never occurred to me that these complications would have life long effects.

When Sam was released to go home from NICU we were to keep him in isolation for six weeks because any illness at that point could be life threatening and at best require another spinal tap. In an attempt to keep Sam from germs that may cause illness Sabrina showered and changed clothes every day when she returned from school and Dick did the same when he returned home from work. I stayed home with Sam.

Most nights I slept on the floor beside Sammy's crib because he was so weak that his cries were barely audible. I was so afraid that he might quit breathing in his sleep. Day and night I cared for Sam and watched him grow stronger.

We were delighted when the six weeks were past and we could be a normal family. Days rolled into weeks and weeks into months. The screaming started. Soon Sam was screaming and throwing himself. He had thrush for months as well as projectile vomiting after each and every feeding. I had a gut feeling that there was something different about my son but well meaning friends would just laugh and tell me that I was old. Or, they would say, "He's just all boy."

Because I believed that there was something so not right with my baby I began reading and reading and reading. I was so angry that Sam had been born with miconium aspiration pneumonia and a group B strep infection and that he had weighed in at nine pounds fifteen ounces the day after my obstetrician had assured me that I would have a nice seven to seven and a half pound baby. I believed then and I believe now that if Sam had been born when he weighed seven and a half pounds that he would not have suffered irreversible brain damage from the infection, lack of oxygen or over oxygenation.

My son screamed, threw himself, vomited, and had thrush month after month. My son was just a baby but he was so out of control and I was so very, very angry.

Not only was I angry but I kept thinking that I didn't want this to ever happen to anyone else. It was such a needless, senseless tragedy.

So, I requested a copy of my medical records and read through them over and over. Each and every time I read the notes following my prenatal appointments the tears would stream down my cheeks. For three weeks the notes read: Mother thinks baby is too big; assurance given.

I set up an appointment with Quality Assurance at the medical facility where I had received prenatal care and where Sam was delivered. I wanted to share my experience with them. I wanted them to tell me that this would never happen again. I pleaded with them to never allow this to happen again. Quality Assurance was a lovely, young blond woman who listened and nodded her head and suggested that I speak with the head of obstetrics so an appointment was made for me to meet with him.

My husband accompanied me to the appointment with

the head of obstetrics. Dick sat and listened and watched as this obstetrician let us know that he was a busy man. The young obstetrician that delivered Sam was no longer practicing at that clinic/hospital and when I mentioned it the head of obstetrics let me know that it was none of my business. While I gripped my medical records in my hands I explained why I was there. I pleaded with him to assure me that this would never be allowed to happen to anyone else. He leaned back in his chair and looked me in the eyes and said in an icy voice, "Sometimes when parents are disappointed with their child they look for someone to blame." I wanted to cry. I wanted to run and cry. I would have wanted to rip his heart out—if he had one. I kept my composure and assured him that I was in no way *disappointed* with my son but that I was extremely disappointed with the lack of care that I had received from his staff at that medical facility. I rose and left. I made it into the elevator before bursting into tears.

I had followed the proper channels of communication within the system and no one seemed to care. It was a CYA (cover your ass) program like no other I had ever experienced. It was cut and dried that the medical institution was in no way liable. So, there was no motivation for them to change their standard of care.

TRUTH: Doctors do not know everything. Doctors are not perfect. Paternalistic Medicine is not in the best interest of clients. Patients are consumers of medical care and need to be wise consumers willing to ask good and sometimes hard questions. Consumers must be willing to change providers before it is too late.

THE REFERRAL

Sam never missed a well baby check up. The pediatrician that provided medical care in NICU following Sam's birth continued to be his medical care provider. He was an excellent doctor. He always ended an appointment with, "Do you have any questions?" When he asked if I had questions he looked at me and waited for a response. He seemed to have all the time in the world to answer my many questions as I was trying desperately to understand my son. Sam was just a little boy but he was so out of control.

During every appointment Dr. Goode reviewed safety precautions with me. I always wondered if the safety lessons were standard for all well baby checks or if they were a result of Sam's perpetual motion and accompanying bruises from frequent falls that warranted the safety reminders.

I always read to Sammy and stroked his head while we waited for the doctor. This calmed him and seemed to limit his excessive activity.

This day while Dr. Goode examined Sam I asked many questions while Sammy squirmed and howled. I asked about tantrums, picking of skin and clothing, headstanding, biting, eating habits, head butting, runny nose, coughing, not sleeping, and drooling. Dr. Goode addressed each of my concerns but he didn't seem to pick up on my urgency. How could he? I was the one living the nightmare. Dr. Goode saw Sammy for approximately fifteen minutes monthly or bi-monthly. How could he possibly know?

Dr. Goode had tongue depressors in his shirt pocket and Sammy kept reaching for them during his exam. When Dr. Goode finished examining Sammy he bent toward Sam and handed him one of the tongue depressors. With bullet speed

Sammy grabbed all of the depressors from Dr. Goode's pocket and flung them about the room.

Dr. Goode smiled at me and then wrote a referral for Sammy to see a well respected psychologist. This referral was the first of many, many referrals to various specialists.

TRUTH: Doctors observe a patient for ten to fifteen minutes per appointment. An isolated symptom does not indicate an illness, disorder or handicap. Many symptoms occurring simultaneously indicate something out of the ordinary which can mean an illness, disorder, or handicap.

SURVIVAL

It was a dark, cold, winter night when I drove nearly an hour one way to attend a PACER meeting. I had never heard of PACER but I learned that it was a parent advocacy support group. Although I had never thought of myself as needing an advocate I knew that I needed to learn how to access help for Sam.

The two women facilitating the meeting started the meeting by introducing themselves. They were both from a city nearly seven hours from the rural community where the meeting was held. They were both mothers of adult handicapped children. They were articulate, knowledgeable, positive women.

After introducing themselves they asked those of us attending the meeting to introduce ourselves. Our introduction was to include our name, why we were there, (teacher, paraprofessional, parent, etc.) and a goal.

When it was my turn I heard my voice say, "My name is Barb Smot. I am the mother of a handicapped child and my goal is survival." I heard some snickers after I stated my goal but I couldn't have been more serious. Sammy could be up and running for thirty-six hours without sleep and I was exhausted.

It was a surreal experience. I heard my voice saying that I was the mother of a handicapped child but it was like I wasn't there. I surely didn't want to be there but I knew that I needed help with my out of control child.

I don't remember much about the meeting beyond my introduction but I left the meeting with a packet of papers explaining the legal rights of handicapped children. The handouts included PACER contact telephone numbers.

I cried all the way home. I had a label and my son had a label. I know that I had never said it and I don't think that I

9

had even thought it but I had introduced myself as the mother of a handicapped child. My goal sounded simple. Survival.

What would it take to survive? I had no idea but it was consuming me.

TRUTH: I am the mother of a handicapped child. I will always be the mother of a handicapped child. I will survive.

MRS. BABY BEAR

Prior to obtaining my MRS. Degree I laughingly referred to farmsteads with two houses as "Papa Bear/Baby Bear Operations". I got married my senior year in college so my MRS. preceded my BS degree by a few months. Following graduation we moved *home* to the farm. Yes, I married a Baby Bear and we lived one quarter of a mile from my all seeing and all knowing in-laws. Was I lucky, or what?

My husband and I taught school during the day and farmed nights and week-ends. We worked long and hard so that we could afford a family.

It was an early spring the year that Sabrina joined our family. I experienced contractions all day Saturday and since I was past my due date I knew that it was the real thing. I didn't sleep all night and by morning the contractions were half an hour apart.

Dick was an experienced farmer and he told me that first calf heifers always take longer so he went to the field to seed.

When my contractions were fifteen minutes apart I got into the car and went to find Dick. I suggested that we head for the hospital which was about an hour from our home. He agreed to shut down the tractor and go home to shower all the while mumbling something about first calf heifers. After Dick showered and I put gas in the car we were on our way to the hospital. I was going to deliver our first child and I was so excited that I couldn't keep track of the time between contractions but I hinted to Dick that he should drive a little faster. When we arrived at the city where I was to deliver our baby Dick remembered that McDonald's was having its Grand Opening and that cheeseburgers were two for the price of one. I didn't think that I looked like I wanted a cheeseburger but to McDonald's we went. Dick seemed perplexed when I opted to stay in the car while he got his cheeseburgers. Before leaving me to go inside to get his cheeseburgers he reminded me again that first calf heifers always take longer.

Well, Dick was right. We arrived at the hospital early Sunday afternoon and Sabrina wasn't born until that night. I had been in labor for almost two days, endured natural childbirth, and had produced what was without a doubt the most perfect and beautiful baby girl the planet earth had ever seen. I had been a key player in what was nothing short of a miracle. To top it off, I had lived to tell about it.

The following day my mother-in-law appeared in my room and asked, "Was Dick disappointed that it wasn't a boy?" followed by, "We don't have any misshapen heads on our side of the family. Do you have misshapen heads on your side of the family?" (Sabrina had a pressure bump on her head from the long labor.)

Sabrina was perfect. She was beautiful, cute, adorable, smart, and just plain perfect. (Did I mention that she was our first child?) Before she was six months old she was diagnosed with congenital hip dislocation on both sides. The orthopedic specialist didn't know if Sabrina would be able to walk without surgeries and she left the diagnostic appointment in a restrictive harness and an eighteen month treatment plan.

My mother-in-law's comment concerning the congenital hip dislocation was, "We don't have any cripples on our side of the family. Do you have any cripples on your side of the family?"

Sammy's birth insured a continuation of the family name and I thought that I had done the family proud. However, following Sam's birth there were years of medical appointments resulting in multiple and varied diagnoses during which time my mother-in-law asked, "We don't have any retarded people on our side of the family. Do you have any retarded people in your family?"

TRUTH: I never nominated her for Mother-in-law of the Year Award.

THE RINGMASTER

Early in Sammy's life I recognized the need for a coordinator for our three ring circus. I knew that I needed help because the demands at home were so great that I could barely keep my head above water, so to speak.

There were so many nuances such as sensory integration dysfunction, echolalia, multiplex-developmental disorder, and the myriad of allergies. What type of specialists should see Sam and where were they to be found?

During one of Sam's routine physical exams I asked Dr. Goode if he would be the coordinator for Sam's needs. He graciously agreed to be our coordinator. He would be the ringmaster of our three ring circus. I already had file folders for various doctors and I knew that there would be more.

As I took Sam from one specialist to another trying to figure out just what made him tick I would learn about other specialists. I was desperate for a diagnosis and a cure. I located specialists near and far and I hauled Sam to see them which was no easy feat. I felt like I was floundering in my ignorance but I couldn't give up. There was appointment after appointment after appointment and there were almost as many diagnoses as appointments.

During this time I kept expecting help. After all, I had asked Dr. Goode to be our coordinator so why wasn't he coordinating? Just exactly what I expected of him I do not know but it became obvious to me that I was the coordinator. I was the ringmaster for this three ring circus. I was reading, attending seminars, ferreting out specialists who might be able to help us, and hauling Sammy to appointments.

As sleep deprived as I was, I was the ringmaster. I am the ringmaster. I will be the ringmaster until I die.

TRUTH: No one loves my son as much as I love him. No one has the vested interest in his success that I have.

ANGELS

I used to have a life. In fact, I had a job when Sam was born. Since I hadn't planned for the NICU followed by isolation at home I hadn't arranged for a babysitter to come into our home. In spite of my lack of planning I couldn't have found a more competent, kinder, more dedicated care person than Doris. She was a grandma who had the patience of a saint. Not only did she care for Sam but she played Monopoly with Sabrina whenever Sam slept.

Sam had projectile vomiting after each and every feeding so I never dressed for work until after Doris had arrived and taken Sam from my arms. When I returned from work Doris was always wearing whatever Sam had been fed and she would just smile like she didn't mind. Dr. Goode, Sam's pediatrician, was not concerned about the projectile vomiting because Sam was in the ninety-nine percentiles in both height and weight.

Since my work schedule was flexible that meant that Doris' work schedule was flexible and we worked around each other's commitments. Doris became more like a family member than an employee. I was so fortunate to have such a competent, reliable, and trustworthy person come into my home to care for my children. She loved my children and she charted Sam's wake times, sleep times, what he ate, level of activity, etc.

All too soon Doris found full-time employment with incredible benefits. I couldn't help but be happy for her but I knew that it would be difficult if not impossible to replace her.

When I was able to hire another grandma who was every bit as competent, reliable, loving, and trustworthy I knew that it wasn't luck. Agnes, too, was flexible and willing to work week-ends.

I was still attending out of town meetings for my job as

well as conferences and educational forums about disabilities. I was desperately trying to find out what was wrong with my child.

While attending an Autism Society conference I listened to many parents talk about their experiences with their autistic children. I couldn't believe that there were other parents living what I was living. There were other parents who were sleep deprived. There were other parents who had children who stood on their heads and spun. I was not alone.

My most memorable memory of all conferences and meetings was when I heard a parent say that they had never heard their child say, "I love you." There were many tears in the room as many other parents painfully acknowledged that they had never heard their children say, "I love you." My child was verbal and I realized that I was blessed. Sam had told me many, many times that he loved me. In fact, he told me many times a day that he loved me. His "I love yous" may have been in response to my "I love yous" but nonetheless Sam told me that he loved me and he told me frequently that he loved me. I was blessed.

When I returned from this conference Agnes was gone. She left a note telling me that Sam had run into her with his battery operated jeep and that she needed medical attention.

Dick told me that Agnes' leg looked bad when she left so I called to check on her. I was relieved to learn that she wasn't injured any worse than the broken blood vessels in her leg. She was elevating her leg and alternating heat and cold according to doctor's orders.

Dick and I took Sam to the basement to look at the accident site. Sam hadn't just run into Agnes with his jeep. He had pinned her against a wall and hadn't even let up on the accelerator. When Dick asked Sam why he had run into Agnes Sam replied, "She didn't move." It was a matter of fact statement: "She didn't move." Incredible. Sam's world was so concrete.

Since I no longer had child care and Sam was so out of

control that I was too embarrassed to look for alternate child care arrangements I quit my part time job and stayed home with Sam in an attempt to figure out just what made him tick. (Tick, not tic!)

TRUTH: Handicapped children are a full time job.

DOING PUBLIC

Public with Sammy was always an adventure since his behavior was erratic, impulsive, and uncontrollable.

After Sam toppled the pyramid of Spam cans in our local grocery store I began shopping out of town. That was back when I could be embarrassed.

When we shopped out of town in the big supermarket Sam would often get away from me because he was so heavy that I couldn't get him into the cart seat by myself. If Sam wouldn't cooperate by climbing up on something to get himself into the cart he was a loose cannon.

If Sam chose not to hold my hand and walk with me or help me push our grocery cart he would often run away and find his own grocery cart. Then the fun would begin. Sam would chase me with his cart while he screamed, "You Idiot!" or "I'll kill you!" The first time this happened I was mortified. Not because of the looks that I received from other shoppers but because I couldn't believe what I was hearing. Where had he learned to talk like this? He was never away from me and I didn't use that language so where was get getting it? Sam only watched Disney videos and Sesame Street.

Fortunately there were several grocery stores in the city where we shopped so I didn't need to return to the same store each time we purchased groceries. After several episodes of, "You Idiot" and "I'll kill you!" I was still puzzled.

The puzzle was solved one day while Sam was watching the Disney movie *101 Dalmatians*. It was then that I heard Cruella shriek, "You Idiots," and "I'll kill you!" Sam was doing a perfect imitation. Shortly after that I learned the term "echolalia" which means repeating what you hear. After that it became obvious to me that much of what Sammy said was echolalia and he had an uncanny ability to do it appropriately so that it sounded like it was original.

Due to sensory overload Sam could not walk through a shopping center so if I wanted to go to more than one store we would need to exit, get into the car, and drive to the next store where we would enter from the outside.

On a particularly busy day at Target I had a full cart, Sam was in the seat in the cart, and we were in the check out line. The line was long and not moving very quickly. I could feel a meltdown coming but there wasn't a thing that I could do. I attempted to entertain Sam. When that didn't work I tried to divert his attention but that failed as well. It wasn't long until we were second from the cashier and Sam started to tantrum.

I pulled my full cart out of the line up of carts and walked down an aisle where I convinced Sam to crawl out of the cart so that we could leave. I abandoned the cart of merchandise and exited the store with Sam.

TRUTH: When you take a handicapped child someplace don't think that there may be trouble——KNOW that there will be trouble. Have Plan A, Plan B, Plan C, as well as an escape route.

AM I YOUR FAVORITE, MOM?

Sam wasn't very old when he looked up at me with his big blue eyes and asked, "Who do you like the most, me or Sabrina?" I was taken aback by the question and as usual, I was mentally scrambling to figure out the stimulus for the question along with any extenuating circumstances. Since Sam is often difficult to understand, I am hard of hearing, and I usually need to buy some time I asked my usual, "Would you say that again, please?"

Sam repeated his question as I looked at his angelic face and his innocent eyes. He really wanted to know if he was my favorite child or if Sabrina was my favorite child and I knew that I had better come up with a satisfactory answer PRONTO.

While Sam and I looked deep into each other's eyes the answer quickly came to me. I must have been subconsciously thinking it for a long time because I gave quite an eloquent explanation of my favorite child.

I told Sam that he is my only son and my favorite son and that I had always loved him best. I told Sam that he is my last born child which made him very special. Thus, Sam became my very most favorite son.

I told Sam that Sabrina is my first born child which makes her very special. I told Sam that Sabrina is my only daughter and my favorite daughter and that I had always loved her best. Thus, Sabrina became my very most favorite daughter.

Sam smiled at me. My answer was simple and truthful and Sam appeared to be more than satisfied. I gave Sammy a big kiss/hug and life was good.

TRUTH: Sam is my very most favorite son. Sabrina is my very most favorite daughter.

OUT STANDING...

Out of sheer desperation I discovered that the hum and motion of a moving vehicle were soothing for Sam. So, a nightly drive became part of our routine.

During one of our evening drives Sam had a melt down that resulted in him standing on his head in the back seat and kicking me in the head over the back of the seat. It had been a trying day and my patience were exhausted. I needed time and space to count to ten in order to prevent myself from saying or doing something that I might regret.

We were driving looking at various fields. We farm in rural America in a sparsely populated area. It's not the end of the world but we have a bird's eye view. When I asked Dick to pull over he did so. I opened the truck door and told Sam to get out and take time out. He continued to tantrum and when I attempted to move him out of the truck he held on for dear life.

I peeled Sam's fingers from the door post and pulled him out of the truck. When I told him to stand there for a time out until we returned for him he kicked at me and grabbed onto the door handle of the truck. I peeled his fingers from around the door handle and as Dick drove away from Sam I ran to jump into the truck. We drove to the far end of the field where Dick inspected the crop. When Dick returned to the truck we sat and talked for a short time before turning the truck around to return to Sam.

When the truck was turned around I could see a truck sitting at the distant end of the field. It was sitting right where we had left Sam. How could this be? What did they want? Were they trying to take Sam? No one ever drove on this township road so why, now, was there someone here to observe my poor parenting skills? After all, I had just left my screaming son in the middle of a field.

Dick seemed to be as amused as I was embarrassed. (That was light years ago when I could be embarrassed.) When we arrived at the end of the field two young men from a nearby farm were visiting with a smiling Sam. While I didn't know the young men as well as Dick knew them I had heard of some of their boyhood antics and escapades and this knowledge seemed to relieve some of my embarrassment regarding the current situation.

Following a brief, jovial visit Sam got into the truck. The boys went their way and we went ours.

TRUTH: "Out standing in his field" took on a whole new meaning.

RICOCHET

Impulsive, out of control, perpetual motion, and fearless were accurate descriptors of pre-school Sammy. While those were some of the words that described Sam, "tired" was the all encompassing word that described me.

Sam had escaped my radar screen so I went looking for him. Since he rarely answered when I called his name I looked and looked and looked. When I went out to the garage I thought I heard a noise so I stood still and listened and listened. The noise seemed to be a quiet, hissing sound so I listened some more in an attempt to find the source of the sound.

I walked to the back end of my car and there on the garage floor was Dick's fishing tackle box. It was open and his fillet knife was on the floor beside the box. It didn't take me long to connect the fillet knife with the hissing sound and conclude that Sammy had "filleted" a tire on my car. I was so thankful that he hadn't cut himself that I wasn't even upset about the tire.

A few days later when I couldn't find Sam I looked and looked for him and called his name but to no avail. I went upstairs to his bedroom where I found the ranch style window on the north end of his bedroom open. When I looked out the window into the rain I saw Sammy running around and around the overhang of the house. A wet roof is a slippery roof and I gasped when I saw his fearless antics. I stood close to the window and called, "Sam, you come in the house, now. One, two, three…" (If I ever counted past three there were consequences such as time out or loss of television privileges.) Sam returned to the window where he had exited and crawled back into the house. I explained to Sam how dangerous it was to be on the roof and especially dangerous when it was raining but he just looked at me with his big, blue eyes. That afternoon I nailed all the upstairs windows shut.

Before the week was over I had lost him again and when I searched and searched Sam was no where to be found. There wasn't a sign of Sammy and not a sound heard. I had looked everywhere and out of desperation I peeked into the grand piano and there he was! I knew that if he had bumped the support that held the top of the piano open the weight of the piano top could have killed him. It was years before I propped the piano open.

Sam seemed to ricochet from one danger zone to another. It was during this time that I found a drop in day care business in a nearby city. It was an answer to prayer.

Since the day care had a four hour limit I would check Sam in, return to my car, set the alarm clock, and sleep. When the alarm rang I would take Sam to McDonald's for lunch, return him to the drop in day care, return to my car, set the alarm, and sleep. It was a glorious routine.

All good things must come to an end and so it was with the drop in day care but the few years that it was open definitely contributed to my ability to meet my goal of survival.

TRUTH: FACT is stranger than FICTION. No one could fabricate my reality.

OFF VS. ON

Potty training and bedwetting seem to be symptomatic of the developmentally delayed which often includes those included under the autism umbrella. Sammy was no exception.

What seems light years ago when Sam was a preschooler schools did not accept students who were not potty trained. So, I pushed the bedwetting to the back burner and targeted kindergarten enrollment for successfully completing the course in potty training. Not only did Sammy need to start school where he would be with his peers I needed Sam to start school so that I could sleep.

During the summer of the concentrated potty training course our family went on vacation. Since Dick doesn't believe in planning ahead we didn't have lodging accommodations when we arrived at our destination. Being a tourist haven meant that lodging was scarce during the off season and we were visiting during peak season.

We found a room and that is exactly what it was—a room. THE room was about twelve feet by twelve feet with two single beds against opposite walls with a narrow path between them. At the end of this narrow path that led to the door was another door with a very, very small bathroom. Four of us and two teeny, tiny beds—hmmmmm..... After considerable discussion it was decided that Dick would sleep in one bed, Sammy and I would sleep in the other bed, and Sabrina would sleep on the floor which meant that half of her body was in the bathroom with the other half sprawling out into the narrow path between our beds. Perfect.

Since I awoke in the morning I knew that at some point I must have fallen asleep but I surely didn't feel like I had slept. I knew one thing and one thing only. I was wet which meant that Sammy was wet and the little, teeny bed was wet.

TRUTH: As my brother once told me, "It is better to be pssst off than pssst on." I knew that he was right like nobody else could have.

YES, TWO TIMES

Before Sabrina started kindergarten I shared with her the wonder of reproduction and sex. I did it only because I wanted to be the one to tell her and I wanted her to know that she could ask me anything, anytime. I didn't want her to learn about sex on the bus or playground. I wanted Sabrina to know that sex was a gift from God. Although I thought she was young, it worked out well.

Sammy was a different story. He seemed to have no interest in what he pronounced, "sax". I had placed some age appropriate and tasteful children's books on his shelf and he had never asked to have them read. We had toured the cattle and he had observed breeding but he had never asked any questions and seemed totally uninterested. We had a cat that had kittens and he showed no interest in anything except the kitties.

When Sammy came home from school one day with a message in his notebook telling me that the school nurse was going to be at school that week to talk with Sam's class about growing up I decided that it was time for me to share with Sammy the wonder of sex and reproduction. I also wanted Sammy to know that if he ever had questions that he could talk to me about anything. If I didn't have answers then we would find them together. So, I planned my little presentation and I practiced in front of a mirror. I knew that it needed to be a short and simple presentation if Sammy was to be able to attend and understand.

I felt full of confidence when I approached Sammy for our little talk. I was so prepared and felt so good about my message that the teacher in me was thinking that it would have been a great lesson to video and share. I had visual aids from some of

29

the tasteful artwork in the little books that I had ever so carefully placed on Sam's bookshelf years earlier. When I had shared all that I thought was appropriate I smiled at Sammy and asked him if he had any questions. He looked up at me, smiled, and asked, "So, have you and Dad ever had *sax?*"

TRUTH: If it can be misunderstood it will be misunderstood. To everything there is a season.......This was not it.

CRASH?

When Dr. Goode referred me to see the psychologist, Dr. Earre, he didn't refer Sam. He referred me. I thought that this was a bit unusual but I was really too tired to think so I just showed up for the appointment.

When Dr. Earre asked me why I was there I told him that I didn't really know since I was the only normal one in my family. That must have been a red flag for the doctor.

After a fairly short visit Dr. Earre asked if I would take a written test for assessment purposes and I agreed to do so. The test was lengthy but since it was multiple guess and true or false it was easy.

At my next appointment Dr. Earre presented me with my assessment results. According to the assessments I was clinically depressed. Since I didn't have a clue what that meant Dr. Earre told me that if I was a college student that I would need to drop out of school because I wouldn't be able to function. College had been "a piece of cake" compared to my current existence.

Dr. Earre suggested that I begin taking an anti-depressant and that I get some real sleep. He even went so far as to suggest that Dick take some night duty so that I could relax and sleep. I went home and filled my prescription and waited for the magical happy feeling that never came.

Although I think that I started feeling better I was definitely more tired. I couldn't get enough rest. So, after a period of time when I was still feeling tired I quit taking the medication.

Some time later while Sam and I were traveling home from a grocery shopping trip that had been particularly challenging I was thinking and thinking and thinking about how I was going to survive this life of mine when I had a less than brilliant idea.

I was meeting a semi truck and I thought about pulling over the center line and ending it all. I was absolutely shocked that I would think of anything so blatantly *sick*. I knew that even if I had pulled in front of the semi that with my luck we wouldn't have been killed but only crippled for life. I also knew that there was a reason that Dr. Earre had prescribed anti-depressants for me and that I needed to be taking them. If I didn't take care of myself I couldn't take care of anyone and everyone else.

TRUTH: I used to have a handle on life but I think it broke off.

YESSSSSSSSSSSSSSSSSS

Following Dr. Goode's referral Dick, Sam, and I entered Dr. Earre's waiting room to register to see this reputable psychologist. I had read in several books that doctor appointments are about fifteen to twenty minutes in length and that many children do not show the symptoms and/or behaviors for which they are there. Since making the appointment to see Dr. Earre I had worried that Sam would act "normal" and our trip would be a waste of time.

We were led from the registration desk to an exam room where Dick, Sam, and I were to wait for Dr. Earre. I had brought books and toys to entertain Sam so that he didn't destroy the exam room. Luckily, I did not need to entertain nor distract Sam. Much to my relief and actual delight, it didn't take Sammy long to find his own entertainment.

Dr. Earre's exam room had a desk and chair on one end of the room, a sofa along a wall, and a rocking/revolving chair in the corner. In no time flat Sammy was standing on his head on the chair in the corner and using his feet against the walls to propel himself and the chair in circles at approximately sixty-five miles per hour. Perfect.

As we waited for Dr. Earre Sam didn't slow down and I could see perspiration on his face but I didn't even try to stop him or slow him down. This was why I had him here and this is exactly what I wanted the doctor to see.

Dr. Earre entered the room and introduced himself and smiled at the blur in the corner as he sat down. Sammy didn't falter. Around and around and around he went. As I explained to Dr. Earre that this was typical behavior as well as other behavior concerns Sam kept up the speed and rhythm. He looked like a human top as he spun around and around.

It took no time at all for Dr. Earre to diagnose Sammy

with ADHD (Attention Deficit Hyperactive Disorder) and write us a prescription for Ritalin. Ritalin was the first in a long line of drugs prescribed for Sammy. .

ADHD was the first of many diagnoses. From ADHD we went to TS (Tourette Syndrome) to multi-plex developmental disorder (I think the term is used when they don't know what to diagnose), to PDD (pervasive developmental disorder) to autism, to Asperger's syndrome (high functioning autism), to NVLD (nonverbal learning disorder) with executive function brain dysfunction.

Can you believe it? One little boy and all those diagnoses. After Tourette Syndrome the labels lost their shock value. I didn't care what we called "it", I just wanted to know what we were going to do about "it". I was living with "it" and it wasn't easy being Sammy and it wasn't easy being me. "It" just wasn't easy.

When we left the clinic I was emotionally, mentally, and physically drained but I had a smug feeling as in, "Yessssssssssssssssssss, he did it!" Sam had been Sam and someone else had seen him in action. In fact, a doctor had seen Sam's perpetual motion and had made a diagnosis and had given us a prescription to make this perpetual motion go away. I had prayed for a diagnosis and we got one.

As I attempted to put Sam in his car seat he kicked me in the head so hard that I saw stars. It wasn't a mean kick (I didn't think) but it was a kick that nearly knocked me out cold. That was Sam.

TRUTH: Be careful what you pray for; you might just get it.

WHAT IF HE WAS YOUR SON?

Sam's first grade teacher was a friend of mine. She had a son the same age but attending a different school. I vividly remembered the day that our sons went through pre-school assessments. She enthusiastically headed to a telephone to tell her husband how well their son had done. I went home in tears.

Sam slept much of first grade. When demands were too great for Sam he would simply shut down and sleep. He didn't cause any problems but he didn't learn.

I read to Sam daily but Sam wasn't reading. Sam practiced printing the letters of the alphabet at home but there was little if any improvement in his ability to form the letters.

During the final parent/teacher conference of first grade Sam's teacher (my friend) showed us some of Sam's school work and some art projects. She was smiling and speaking so positively about Sam. Finally I asked her if her son could read. She responded affirmatively. I asked her if her son could print.

She responded affirmatively. I asked her if Sam was her son if she would be concerned and she responded affirmatively.

TRUTH: The same emotional attachments and familiarity that permeate a small community making it a safe haven make it especially difficult, however necessary, to tell parents painful news regarding their children.

WELCOME

Judging from our first encounters I would never have guessed that our families would become long haul friends.

Dick was in Lou's office when Sammy and I entered the bank. I held Sammy's hand firmly in mine and I had my paperwork in order so that all I needed to do was hand the papers to the teller. The last time Sam got away from me in the bank he ended up in the vault.

Dick saw me and came out to invite Sam and me to meet our community's new banker. Sam and I were barely through the office door when Sammy wriggled away from me. He proceeded to climb up the front of a steel file cabinet using the drawer handles for steps. After a few trips up and down the file cabinet Sam was content to sit on top of the cabinet like a bird on a perch as he looked down on us. He was so pleased with himself. His smile was angelic.

Fast forward a few weeks and Sam and I are at home when there is a knock, knock, knocking at the door. I opened the door and greeted Lou and invited him inside. While Lou stood on the end of the entry rug Sammy made a run for him from the opposite side of the room. Lou smiled a broad smile when he saw Sammy approaching with such enthusiasm. The smile was short lived when Sam punched Lou in the crotch with all his might. Lou dropped to his knees on the rug. I'm not sure but I think that I was able to contain my laughter about the same time Lou was able to get to his feet.

Welcome!

TRUTH: Impulsivity equals unpredictability.

CAMP VOCABULARY

For a variety of reasons Sammy attended summer camp for seven summers. Sam needed social experiences and he needed to gain some independence skills but I believe that camp was initially all about respite for me and I was and am definitely okay with that.

Prior to Sam's departure each summer or during his absence I would make two or three target goals. Sam wasn't able to make a change in behaviors unless he had a physical break so it was after his month long absence that we could work on behavior modifications.

His first summer the number one goal was to get Sam out of our bed. Each and every night I would read Sam a story while I rocked him in his rocking chair, say prayers with Sam, and tuck Sam into his own bed. Sometime within the next few hours Sam would creep downstairs and crawl into our bed next to me. Since I knew where he was and what he was doing I hadn't protested much. I knew that it could be worse. However, I knew that Sam needed to sleep in his own bed by himself.

I drove eight hours one way to get Sam after a month at camp. He got stuck on one negative experience and tantrumed for the first two hours. He fell asleep and when he woke he was in better humor.

When we arrived home Sam was happy to see his pets, his sister, and his dad. He still didn't have anything good to say about camp but I was well rested or so I thought before the long, grueling drive accompanied by Sam's tantrum. I was ready to implement the new sleeping arrangements.

That night after putting Sammy to bed I went to bed. Before I crawled into bed I shut and locked our bedroom door.

It wasn't long until I heard the door latch softly rattle.

Then it rattled a little louder and a little louder and pretty soon Sam was kicking the door yelling, "Open door. Let me in."

I knew that if I opened the door all would be lost so I sat inside the door with tears rolling down my cheeks while Sam stood outside the door pounding, kicking, and yelling. This went on until I thought Sam had exhausted himself and fallen asleep on the floor. About that time I heard something but I wasn't sure what it was so I flipped on the light to find a piece of paper that had been slid under the door.

In Sam's unique scrawl were the words: "You basturds, I hate you."

Sam had definitely expanded his vocabulary at camp that summer.

TRUTH: The pain of change often requires an accompanying leap of faith.

ALOHA!

It just so happened that Sam attended his first summer camp the year that Sabrina graduated from high school. It just so happened that my mother gave Sabrina a trip to Hawaii for her graduation gift. Not only did she take Sabrina to Hawaii for two weeks but she allowed Sabrina to take a friend to Hawaii with them. It just so happened that Sabrina chose me to accompany her and Grandma to Hawaii.

So, instead of sitting at home fretting about Sam's absence while he attended camp and imagining his camp existence I was hanging out in a tropical paradise with two of my favorite people.

Leaving Sam at camp was likely more traumatic for me than for Sam. We had packed Sam's belongings carefully using the camp provided check list. Since Sam seemed to have no concept of time we made a calendar so that he could check off the days until I would return for him. In spite of the preparations we made for Sam's camp experience I was not a bit happy about leaving Sam for thirty days knowing that I could have no contact with him other than mail.

Speaking of mail, I had self addressed stamped envelopes and enclosed a lined sheet of paper in each envelope that started, "Dear Mom and Dad". I had prepared letters and cards to be mailed to Sam. I decided to send mail to Sam Mondays, Wednesdays, and Fridays while he was at camp so I got everything ready with sticky notes on each showing the date to be mailed and left them all at the post office to be sent while I was gone. (Another advantage of living in Small Town America.)

Dick accompanied Sam and me to camp the first summer. I hugged Sammy before turning to leave and I know that the tears were running down my cheeks before I was fully pivoted away from his view. It was a long, sad trip home.

A few days later I was in Hawaii and it was a great diversion. Three generations of women just hanging out and bonding provided us with a lifetime of memories. Many times each day I *wondered* how Sam was doing and Mom and Sabrina would assure me that he was just fine. I spoke with Dick frequently on the telephone and each time I asked if we had received a letter from Sam and each time he told me that we hadn't.

When I returned home we still hadn't received a letter from Sam. It wasn't until just a few days before I was to pick Sam up at the end of the thirty day session that there was a letter from Sam in our mailbox. I was elated when I recognized the self addressed envelope. I ripped it open and read the letter: "Dear Mom and Dad, I am fine. How are you? XXOO, Sam."

Three days later I drove the seven hour route to get Sam. I barely recognized him. His skin was so tan and his hair was shaggy. The clothes that he was wearing didn't match. When he saw me his eyes lit up and he greeted me with a hug. We loaded his duffle bag into the car and headed for home.

I wanted to hear all about Sam's camp experiences. He shared very little before getting stuck on a negative experience which resulted in a tantrum followed by a long nap. When Sam awoke he was a happy boy and the remainder of our trip home was uneventful except for Sam telling me that he had forgotten what I looked like. Every summer after that a photo album made just for camp accompanied the calendar and Sam to camp.

Mom, Sabrina, and I had such a fabulous tropical experience that we decided to make Hawaii an annual event. So, every summer thereafter I took Sam to camp and Mom, Sabrina, and I went to Hawaii for two weeks.

Many times I thought that the two weeks in Hawaii were instrumental in helping me achieve my goal of survival. I had two weeks of rest and relaxation. I slept and slept and slept. There was no, "Hey, Mom.......Hey, Mom.......Hey, Mom....." I was able to let my guard down and relax. It was heaven on earth and I am forever grateful to my mother for this opportunity.

TRUTH: Sometimes girls just need to have **fun!**

NOT THE PERSON
FOR THE JOB

Upon Sam's return from his second summer camp experience he was stuck on one of his cabin counselors. Sam ranted and raved about her yelling and swearing. Sam had always been sensitive to loud noises and voices so I just listened while he vented. When Sam added the following remark to his yelling and swearing rampage I took notice. On what must have been a particularly trying day Geneology, as she was called, had yelled at the boys, "I don't know what I'm doing here. I don't even like kids."

Volume is subjective, swearing is value laden, but telling

kids that you don't like kids is totally unacceptable. I carefully explained to Sammy that the counselor must have had a bad day and that she probably didn't really mean what she had said. I also told Sam that not all people are good candidates for summer camp counselors because of the demands of the job.

I wrote a letter to the camp director expressing Sam's and my concerns. Mr. Camp Director called me on the telephone to ask some questions. Regardless of what all had happened and/or been said, I assured him that Sam didn't have the ability to make up such a comment. At that point in time Geneology was on the list of returning staff for the upcoming summer. I requested that Sam not be in her cabin.

The day that I registered Sam at camp we learned that Geneology had not returned.

This was a clear sign to me that this family owned and run camp was every bit as concerned about the quality of program and staff as they advertised. Sam attended this camp for five summers.

Sam never wanted to go to camp but when he started complaining about camp being the same and that he knew everything I started looking for a different camp.

Fortunately, I was receiving several professional publications about various handicaps. It was in one of these publications that I learned about another camp.

I checked out the camp via the internet, I called and requested brochures and a pre-registration packet, and I visited with the camp director on the telephone. I soon learned that handicapped kids from many states, provinces, and countries attended this camp. Many of them were return campers and that there was a waiting list to get into this camp.

After completing the required forms we waited for an open slot. Again, I set goals to be accomplished at camp and after camp. I made it clear in the pre-registration forms that food was not an issue and that Sam wouldn't be attending camp to expand his culinary horizons.

When Sam returned from camp he was stuck on three things: a cabin counselor had yelled and sworn at the campers, he was required to eat foods that he didn't like in order to get food that he did like, and he was taken on an overnight camping trip where skinny dipping was required.

At that time I was still trying to win the "Parent of the Year" Award so I knew that I needed to follow up on these concerns. I asked Sam lots of questions for verification and then I wrote a letter to the camp director.

Once again, Mr. Camp Director called me to discuss my concerns. Actually, I don't think that he called to discuss concerns. He called to let me know that the counselor was a favorite counselor and that he hadn't yelled or used inappropriate language. He assured me that no one was required to eat anything that they didn't want to eat and he was indignant that anyone would even mention skinny dipping. When I told him that Sam wasn't capable of fabricating skinny dipping because he had no prior knowledge of such an activity Mr. Camp Director asked me to talk to Sam and get back to him.

I did just that. Sam held firm to all three concerns. He said that he had taken pictures of boys skinny dipping but that he couldn't find his camera which didn't surprise me at all.

Following through, I called Mr. Camp Director to affirm that Sam's concerns were valid. We agreed that volume is subjective. We agreed that being "encouraged" to try new foods can be misinterpreted. We did not agree on the skinny dipping issue. Mr. Camp Director held firm that no such thing occurred at his camp. He told me that some campers may have been talking about skinny dipping which is how Sam would have learned the term but no such activity took place at his camp.

Before hanging up the phone I thanked Mr. Camp Director for the time and effort that he had expended investigating Sam's concerns. I told him that his efforts affirmed my belief that his was a quality camp and that Sam would be attending the following summer.

Like other years Sam didn't want to attend camp. Unlike other years, Sam threatened to commit suicide if he had to attend camp. After considerable discussion Sam agreed to attend camp provided that he could choose to attend or not attend summer camps in the future.

When Sam returned from camp he informed me that the yelling and swearing counselor from the previous summer had not returned. The word around camp was that it was because of Sam's mother that the counselor hadn't returned.

Although Sam wasn't stuck on food he did tell me that at one meal they were served a spaghetti dish with lots of veggies. When the bowl was passed around the table the campers were taking spaghetti but leaving the veggies. The counselor at the table told the campers that if they took all the spaghetti that there wouldn't be any spaghetti left. Hmmm...I began to laugh and I laughed and laughed and laughed. I told Sam that the counselor must have been on break from NASA. "If you take all the spaghetti there won't be any spaghetti left." Sam laughed and I laughed. We still laugh about the spaghetti. Laughing is good.

Again Sam was wild about the skinny dipping. He told me that skinny dipping was "sick" and "gay" and that he refused to do it.

While Sam was at camp each summer I cleaned his room and removed clothing that he had outgrown. During my annual cleaning routine I happened upon a couple single use cameras and had them developed. One of the cameras just happened to contain the camp photos from the previous summer and guess what? Sam had photos of bare butts swimming. Bare butts swimming equals skinny dipping.

When I showed the photos to Sam he went wild. He knew that there had been skinny dipping and now he knew that I knew that there had been skinny dipping. He had proved it with his photos.

Seeing the photos must have brought back memories because Sam told me that the counselors on the overnight camping trip had told the campers that if they told anyone about the skinny dipping that their field trip money would be taken and no one would ever know.

Wow.

This was the end of Sam's summer camp experiences. Lest you be left to believe that there were only negative experiences let me hasten to tell you just the opposite. Sam's camping sessions provided key social activities as well as other opportunities that he wouldn't have otherwise experienced. Sam learned to use a bow and arrow, he learned gun safety and marksmanship, he improved his nonexistent swimming skills, he knee boarded and got up on water skis, he danced his first dance, and he was responsible for his personal belongings and grooming.

Camps had provided much needed learning opportunities for Sam.

TRUTH: My son is so vulnerable. If I am required to choose I will always err in believing him rather than err in not believing him. I will advocate for him and I will teach him to advocate for himself.

SWIMMING TO
IMPERFECTION

When Sam was old enough to take swimming lessons I enrolled him in the same swimming program that Sabrina had attended years earlier. The lessons were given in a small lake at a little park several miles from our farm.

During the years that Sabrina took lessons Moms visited on the beach while they sunned themselves and we were always sad when the weeks quickly passed and swim lessons were over.

When Sam took swimming lessons I wasn't as relaxed as I was when Sabrina took lessons. Sam had absolutely no fear of anything including water. Although I spent my time on the shore vigilantly watching Sam's every move there were still occasions when Sam had to be pulled out from deep water spitting and sputtering.

After nearly drowning and not learning to swim I decided that maybe private lessons in a pool would make Sam a swimmer. So, I took him to a nearby community for private lessons. I doubt if the teenager giving swimming lessons knew much about children and likely nothing about handicapped children. These lessons didn't make Sam a swimmer, either.

Through the educational system we met an adaptive special education teacher that gave private swimming lessons in a city not too far away and she agreed to work with Sam. For three summers I took Sam to her for private swimming lessons. I couldn't bear to watch the lessons because she knew just how long Sam could be under water without drowning and she would let him stay under for that time before pulling him out and letting him spit water and gasp for air. I had great respect for her knowledge, her techniques, equipment, etc, but I couldn't watch. Sam was not able to coordinate the upper part of his body with the lower part of his body so swimming was nearly impossible for Sam. He did learn to float on his back— if he could relax.

Sam took swimming lessons all seven summers that he attended camps and he never progressed beyond the beginner level of the Red Cross Swimming Program.

TRUTH: Although Sam is not an Olympic swimmer the lessons did provide him with great exercise opportunities along with creating an environment where he could safely have fun in the water.

TWO FOR ONE?

Since Sabrina had been an only child for nine years I was concerned that she not feel neglected or that she was demoted in status in the family with Sammy's arrival. While I carefully planned the transitioning of a new baby into our family I had absolutely no idea how all consuming Sammy would be. He exhausted me physically and mentally.

The more time consuming Sammy became the more determined I was to keep Sabrina's life as "normal" as possible. I attended all of her extra-curricular activities, I kept our home open to friends and family, we traveled for piano lessons and braces on her teeth, we enjoyed family vacations, and over a period of years we hosted three exchange students.

Sabrina was a bright, energetic, gregarious young woman with such great potential and I wanted to give her every possible opportunity to be the best that she could be. I wanted her to be happy.

Being Sabrina's mother, Sammy's mother, and Dick's wife was beyond all consuming not to mention being an only daughter. I didn't want to let anyone down.

Trying to "do it all" kept me exhausted and stressed. One day while Sammy slept following one of his tantrums I sat in tears. Sabrina looked at me and said, "Mom, you need to institutionalize Sam." I looked at Sabrina through my tears in utter disbelief. When I asked Sabrina why she thought Sammy should be institutionalized she replied, "If you don't institutionalize Sam you will need to be institutionalized. Why sacrifice two lives for one life?"

Regardless of how hard I had tried, I hadn't kept things "normal" for Sabrina. I initially thought that her comment was heartless but I came to realize that her comment was a result of fear—fear of losing her mother.

I knew that I needed to try harder and I knew that Sam needed a med change.

TRUTH: Having a handicapped sibling poses challenges, fears, and frustrations unique to that relationship.

STUCK

Although not all autistic individuals perseverate it is a common symptom. Perseveration is an impressive sounding word for getting stuck.

Sam got stuck on food. Sometimes he would eat yogurt for weeks at a time. Sometimes he wanted pancakes for breakfast for months. As a preschooler he went for six weeks eating only bananas, toast with honey, and milk.

If Sam wanted to do something, know something, or get something he would ask over and over. Because he would ask the same questions day after day, week after week, month after month, and sometimes year after year there were times when I felt like I was being pecked to death.

Sam got stuck on Chihuahuas. I don't know why but I think that it happened around the time that Taco Bell had an extensive advertising campaign with a Taco Bell Chihuahua. While Sam would never even think about eating anything from Taco Bell he still *needed* every Chihuahua that Taco Bell sold. Sam relentlessly asked for a real Chihuahua. It didn't matter that we had a dog and a cat and a gerbil. Sam wanted a Chihuahua. Whenever I went anyplace Sam would ask me to bring him a Chihuahua.

Sam asked me to bring him a Chihuahua from Hawaii. I told him that I had never seen Chihuahua in Hawaii. While window shopping in Lahaina I saw a bobble head Chihuahua wearing a grass skirt and lei. I immediately entered the store and purchased the bobble head along with the Hawaiian wardrobe. When I returned home Sam was delighted with his Chihuahua but that didn't stop him from asking for a Chihuahua.

Several years later Grandma gave Sam a stuffed, singing Chihuahua for Christmas. The singing Chihuahua was the highlight of Sam's gifts and it proudly sits on a shelf in his bedroom next to his other Chihuahuas. Sam still asks for a Chihuahua.

Getting stuck and rituals seem to go hand in hand. We have been eating pizza for our Sunday noon meal for as long as I can remember. I am not certain how the ritual started but I think that it was during the time we attended church in a nearby community where there was a convenience store that sold Hot Stuff Pizza.

Sunday School ended at noon and we were hungry so it was quick and easy to get a pizza. To begin with Sam would call and place the order for the pizza to be ready at noon. After a couple years of phone practice I decided that Sam also needed practice handling money so I would give Sam money and he would go into the store to get the pizza by himself. This was great for Sam. He was totally responsible for ordering the pizza as well as paying for it—both life skills.

Since pizza for Sunday lunch was established there was no deviating. After we returned to our country church we continued to order pizza before going to church and then drove to the nearby town to get the pizza after church.

The church has an annual business meeting in January followed by a potluck dinner. Sam's body got rigid and he quivered when the scheduled potluck dinner was mentioned so I knew that we needed pizza because that's what we did on Sundays.

When Pastor asked Sam why we weren't staying for potluck dinner Sam was quick to tell him that Sundays we ate Hot Stuff pizza and drank pop. After that Pastor made sure that Sam's favorite Hot Stuff Pizza and pop were at the pot luck dinner and we attended the pot luck dinners.

TRUTH: Perseveration is symptomatic of autism as well as some other developmental disabilities. Without a sense of humor perseveration could drive a *normal* person over the edge. Our many Chihuahuas all have names: Juan, Pedro, Jose, Speedy, etc.

LAZY, STUBBORN, AND SPOILED

Even though there is research that shows that self contained classrooms with theme teaching are more productive than departmentalized classrooms our school departmentalizes grades four through six. The school staff that supports departmentalization insist that it promotes independence in students and better prepares students for junior high school. In truth, departmentalization is teacher friendly; not student friendly.

Sam's IEP (individual education plan) said that he was to be mainstreamed in fourth grade. This meant that he would attend regular classrooms with his peers with some modifications and supports. A communication notebook went to and from school with Sammy daily and all assignments were written in the notebook.

Math was a difficult subject for Sam so the IEP team decided that it would be best for Sam to have modified assignments meaning that he wouldn't be assigned as many math problems per lesson/assignment.

During the first parent/teacher conference Sam's math teacher told me that Sam was often gazing out the classroom window. He told me that Sam often put his head down on his desk like he was tired. I reminded the teacher that Sam had Asperger's Syndrome and that these were signs of overload.

A short time later an autism specialist visited our school and observed Sam in his classrooms. This autism specialist was the same person that had diagnosed Sam two years earlier. Our regional special education cooperative hired her to offer support services to the member schools.

When the autism specialist met with the math teacher this teacher told the specialist that he had EBD (emotionally and behaviorally disturbed) experience and that Sam was lazy, stubborn, and spoiled and that he would whip him into shape. In his infinite ignorance this teacher had labeled my son "lazy, stubborn, and spoiled".

The autism specialst was a middle aged, assertive woman. She told the math teacher that Sam was autistic and that if he ever tried any of his EBD mumbo jumbo with Sammy that she would have his sorry ass fired.

As a result of this exchange I requested that Sam be removed from this classroom and placed in the special education resource room for his math instruction.

TRUTH: Being paid a teacher's salary does not make a teacher.

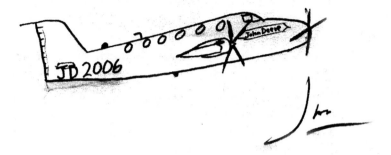

WHEN A TOY IS NOT A TOY

I had always been told that you can tell a lot about a person from the way they treat children, elderly, and animals. I learned something very important about a man that I didn't know well by watching him interact with Sam. I didn't know it at the time but this man would later become a business partner.

As farmers often do, Dick, Sam, and I just dropped in at Bob's and Jane's home. Within minutes of entering their home Sam had found a computer. Jane encouraged Sam to play games on the computer. Although Jane and Bob had no idea how short Sam's attention span was it was no surprise to me when Sam was soon reaching for the John Deere airplane that was sitting on a shelf just out of his grasp.

The shelf was home to box after box containing John Deere toys. Perhaps because I was stressed due to Sam's whining or perhaps I just didn't know better but I had no clue that these were John Deere collectible replicas—NIB (new in box).

Sam continued to reach for the shelf and whine until Bob removed the box containing a John Deere airplane from the shelf and handed it to Sam. I was mortified when Sam ripped the box apart and removed the airplane. The airplane had a moveable propeller and Sam was fascinated by twirling that propeller around and around and around.

When it was time for us to leave which wasn't nearly soon

enough to my liking I had to pry Sam's fingers from the airplane. Sam did not relinquish the plane willingly and he did not leave willingly. Sam's out of control departure was just another fine example of what might be the results of poor parenting.

Less than a week after our visit there was a knock, knock, knocking at our door. When I opened the door there stood Bob with a John Deere toy box in his hand. By the time Bob was through the door Sam was there to investigate. Bob handed the John Deere box containing a new John Deere airplane to Sam whose eyes were sparkling and whose lips were smiling a wide and happy smile.

Bob and Sam have been "buds" since the first John Deere airplane.

I had tears in my eyes when Bob appeared at our door with the "toy" airplane. I have tears in my eyes as I write this because it is so warming to know that there are folks out there who "get it" and even if they don't "get it" they don't judge harshly.

TRUTH: You really can tell a lot about the character of a man from the way he treats children, elderly, and animals. You can tell even more from the way a man treats a handicapped child.

HOPPING HOME

Before the school year started I met with some of the staff in an attempt to ensure Sam's success as well as his safety. I was particularly concerned about the bus ride to and from school since this had been a problem previous years. I had done my homework concerning bussing issues and I suggested any or all of the following: seat assignments, the use of a video camera, and a paraprofessional bus monitor.

Decision makers at school chose to make no changes.

During the following weeks and months Sam returned from school with bruises and scratches and nose bleeds. He complained that he was being hit and kicked during the bus rides.

I always told Sam that he was never to hit anyone. I told him to stay away from kids that weren't nice to him. I told him to use words, not fists. I repeated this guidance to Sammy over and over for years while he was being victimized by his peers.

This year's bus ride seemed to be worse than the preceding year's rides. I had written notes to Sam's teacher in his daily communication notebook regarding the bruises, scratches, and nose bleeds. I had called the principal and I had gone to school to talk with the teacher and principal but nothing changed.

One day at bus time when I was listening for Sam's return I heard the door open followed by a thud. I went to see what was going on only to find Sammy laying on the floor with his shoes tied together. He had fallen over the threshold and landed inside the house. The shoes weren't just tied together. They were knotted and knotted and knotted. Sammy was wet with perspiration. He had hopped home from the bus stop which was just less than one quarter of a mile from our house.

I didn't want Sammy to know how upset I was but I was so furious that I could barely see or hear. When I asked Sammy how his shoe laces got knotted he told me that he was sleeping on the bus and when it was time to get off the bus his shoes were tied together. Sammy didn't think to remove the shoes so he had hopped home with his shoes tied together. Yes, Sammy had hopped a little less than a quarter of a mile because someone had tied his shoes together.

I made a telephone call to the school principal to tell him that Sam had just hopped home from the bus stop because someone had tied his shoes together. I reminded him that this was not an isolated incident and that I had repeatedly asked for help regarding Sam's bus ride. I told him that if I sent my son to school with the bruises and scratches that he came home with that the school would be required by law to report the situation to social services. Then I told him that Sam would not be attending school until changes were made on the bus to ensure Sam's safety.

The following day the principal called me to set up a meeting with me and school personnel. We met the following afternoon after school.

I took Sam's shoes with me to the meeting. I thought that perhaps a visual aid would show the school staff that my son had been victimized and that I was serious about needed changes. I was so angry but I was more hurt than angry. How could anyone be so cruel to Sammy? The shoes were knotted so badly that the laces had to be cut out of the shoes. I cried when I showed Sammy's shoes to the school staff attending the meeting.

It was a quiet meeting. No one, including the head bus driver, seemed to have any suggestions for solutions. They told me that most of the video cameras in the buses didn't work. They told me that there wasn't staff available for monitoring bus rides. They told me that bus drivers needed to watch the road so they couldn't see everything that happened on the bus. Once again I suggested assigned seats. I suggested that Sam have an assigned seat. I told them that I wanted Sam assigned to sit in the front seat on the opposite side from the bus driver so that the driver could see Sam as well as those around him.

Those attending the meeting thought that that this was a brilliant idea. It was to be implemented the following morning.

How could all those well educated staff members with years of experience not be able to come up with a single suggestion to solve this problem while I, the dumb and incompetent parent, presented a simple, common sense solution that I had suggested before the school year started? Amazing.

For the remainder of the school term and the following year Sammy sat in the front seat and there were no more problems on the bus.

TRUTH: Children can and will be cruel. Teachers can and will be apathetic. It is a parent's job to advocate for their child.

THROW THE BALL UP

For years I sat on gymnasium bleachers Saturday mornings watching elementary basketball. When Sabrina participated in elementary basketball and I was a Saturday morning mom in the bleachers I was surrounded by moms of Sabrina's classmates who were my friends. In addition to watching and cheering for our future stars we usually managed some lively and interesting discussions. Before I knew it bleacher time was over and we were on our way home.

Sabrina wasn't particularly athletic but I didn't care. I had high hopes that she would be a concert pianist so the fact that she was born with congenital hip dislocation on both sides leaving her with rotation abnormalities didn't upset me. Sabrina's obvious lack of coordination along with the absence of that athletic, Neanderthal, competitive killer instinct didn't phase me.

Even though my heart was never in basketball I supported the team in their efforts and I encouraged my very most favorite daughter who aspired to be a professional ball player as well as her teammates who had similar aspirations. I encouraged equal playing time for all participants. I always told Sabrina about one positive move of the day and I empathized with her the day that I found her crying in the locker room following a tournament where the coach decided to "put in the scrubs". Sabrina did not think that she was a scrub. I *knew* that Sabrina wasn't a scrub but that's a different story.

When Sammy entered third grade I was not looking forward to Saturday mornings. My body was too old to sit on bleachers for hours at a time. Sam's classmates' parents were much younger than I, and watching Sam *try* to play basketball was so painful.

Sam was uncoordinated so running was difficult to impossible for him. In fact, he never did run. He skipped down the basketball court. Ball handling was a challenge for Sam. Sometimes he made contact with the basketball but more times than not he just slapped the air around the ball. Sam was by far the poorest player on the team. There were a couple other not so talented boys on his team as well so the team never advanced too far in tournament play. In spite of the difficulties of basketball, I believed that Sammy needed the exercise, the ability to follow directions, the team experience, as well as the social interaction. The game of basketball was not the reason for Sammy's participation.

Saturday after Saturday, year after year I traveled to various towns to sit in their gymnasiums and watch elementary basketball. After all, I was a good mother and good mothers support their children's efforts.

One cold Saturday morning I drove over an hour to get to my spectator seat at the basketball game. The gym was cold, the bleachers were cold, and I was cold but I watched and cheered. It was a boys' and girls' tournament that day so there were lots of basketball players, parents, grandparents, and siblings watching the games. Some families actually found elementary basketball entertaining and enjoyable.

This particular Saturday long after the part of my anatomy on which I sit had become numb the game ended with a most interesting play. With only seconds remaining on the clock someone panicked and passed the ball to Sam. He "body caught" the ball and stood with his back to the basket hugging the ball tightly. Spectators were cheering as the seconds counted down to the buzzer when the principal's loud, clear, familiar voice was heard, "Throw the ball up". Sam did just that. With his back to the basket he threw the ball up into the air over his back. It was an amazing sight. The crowd was silent for a split second and then the laughing started.

Although I was a couple years beyond allowing anything or anybody to embarrass me I did have a sick feeling in my stomach as I smiled and said to those around me, "He did just as he was told."

Sam's world was literal and concrete. "Throw the ball up," was a simple command that would have told most ball players to pivot, line up, aim for the basket, and shoot. Sam was *not* most basketball players.

TRUTH: Literal and concrete interpretation requires people to say what they mean and mean what they say.

STOP

We are a family of snowmobile riders. Snowmobiling seems to be one of the few benefits of living in the frozen north where we have winter for a minimum of six months each year.

When Sam was twelve years old we obtained an ATV rule book and enrolled Sam in an ATV training class. I read the manual over and over to Sam. He attended the classes and surprised us by passing the test and becoming a licensed ATV driver.

Sam had driven a Kitty Cat when he was small and now that he had a license he advanced to an Indy Light. Sam was so proud of his bright red Indy Light.

One Sunday afternoon Sammy and his father decided to go riding on the trails. They got all suited up and left. After a few hours they returned and when they came through the door there was definitely disagreement in the air. I could hear bickering and yelling and stomping. When I went to investigate, Sammy let go with a tirade about his father causing an accident.

Sammy had crashed his snowmobile because his father had stopped in front of him. I asked questions hoping to clarify what seemed to be conflicting stories. Dick said that Sam had run his snowmobile into the back end of his machine. Sammy said that Dick hadn't given him the sign to stop. Before they left Dick had told Sam that when he wanted him to stop he would hold his right hand up to give the stop sign. I finally asked Sammy if he hadn't seen that his dad was stopped. His father interjected that he wasn't even on the machine but standing beside it. How could Sam not have seen it? Sammy repeated, "You didn't give me the sign." Dick's snowmobile was parked with no rider. Sam saw the stopped machine but crashed his snowmobile into the back of the parked machine because Dick didn't hold up his right hand to signal Sammy to stop.

A few weeks and twelve hundred dollars worth of repairs later Sam and his dad went snowmobiling. Again, Sam crashed his snowmobile into the back of his dad's snowcat. Again his dad was stopped but this time Sammy didn't see the stopped snowmobile because he was looking at something off the trail. Moral of the story: if you are in front of Sammy, don't stop!

TRUTH: Many individuals with developmental disorders are not flexible. Make a plan and follow the plan.

MOWING TO PERFECTION

Mowing the lawn was my job because I wanted it done well. I didn't just want it mowed well, I will admit that I wanted it mowed my way.

We have a very large yard with much of the front yard being open. There are a couple landscaping beds at the bottom of the hill by the house and some trees on the south end of the house. Other than those beds and trees it is just lawn. I like to mow the lawn north and south one mowing, an angle the next mowing, east and west the next mowing, an angle the next, and then repeat the pattern.

I had always been in charge of mowing. Our daughter had sat in my lap while I drove the mower for years so when she was old enough to take the lawnmower safety course offered by the county extension service I assumed that she would take over the lawn mowing duties. Sabrina took the class and learned how to change oil on the mower and how to change spark plugs but she didn't seem to learn how to mow.

When Sabrina started mowing the lawn I told her about my mowing strategy that I described earlier and expected her to follow it. When I would look out the window sometimes she was driving in circles! There was no circular pattern in my mowing strategy. I would go upstairs in the house and look out the window down onto the lawn only to see chaos. It was obvious that Sabrina and I had different standards. I wanted the lawn to be manicured and she just wanted to get the job done.

I won't say that she didn't care but I know that her heart and mind were not in or on lawn mowing. In fact, one time when her father drove by on the road he noticed that she was not only mowing in road gear but that she didn't have the blades engaged. He was kind enough to stop and share his observations so that she would slow down and engage the blades. Blades are good when mowing grass.

Although I shared my mowing strategy repeatedly with Sabrina it just never happened that way when she mowed. I would look out the upstairs window and see bits and pieces of lawn mowed and other bits and pieces of lawn not mowed and absolutely no rhyme or reason to the mowing. The end result was not the manicured yard that I expected and wanted.

Rather than make this a battle of wills I took back the lawn mowing duties. (At that time in my life I was more concerned that Sabrina become a concert pianist and I was willing to pick my fights and the lawn wasn't one of them.)

Sam was born in October so he was seven months old when the lawn needed to be mowed. I cradled him in my arm and mowed. With the mower we had at that time it took approximately six hours to mow the lawn so Sammy and I spent many hours together on the lawnmower.

Summer after summer Sammy and I mowed the lawn. Each year he was a little bigger and a little heavier but he was always in my lap and always went right to sleep. The motion and noise of the mower lulled Sam to sleep and we mowed the lawn like that until Sammy was so big and heavy that my legs would go to sleep from his weight.

Around that time Sammy was old enough to take the lawnmower safety class that the county extension service offered—the same class that Sabrina had taken years earlier. I enrolled Sam and took him to class so that he could learn how to mow the lawn. He passed the course the first summer but I knew that he wasn't ready to mow the lawn. I knew that he wouldn't mow to my specifications so he continued to ride with me while I mowed.

The following summer I enrolled Sammy in the lawnmower safety class again and he learned mower safety, maintenance, and operation again. After passing the course for the second time I was ready to relinquish the lawn mowing duties to Sam. After all, he had been riding on the mower with me for eleven summers. He knew the routine.

I explained my mowing strategy to Sammy. I didn't expect him to remember it so I told him each time he mowed how I wanted him to mow: north and south, angle, east and west, angle, and so forth. After verbally explaining the mowing strategy for the day to Sammy I used a dry erase board and drew a diagram of the mowing strategy to make certain that he understood what to do. I didn't expect Sammy to mow close to the house so I mowed the first couple passes and then turned the mower over to Sam.

About that time Dick pulled into the driveway and as we stood in the driveway talking we heard an awful racket. It sounded like rocks going through the mower blades. Although I was afraid of being hit by flying rocks, Dick and I headed for the noise. By the time we got there the noise had quit. In fact, the mower had quit. Sam had driven the mower into a landscape bed and into a tree, shooting landscape rocks through the mower as he went.

When I asked Sammy why he had driven the mower into the landscape bed he didn't have an explanation. We got the mower back onto the lawn, painted the spot on the tree that had been debarked and chalked it up to experience.

When I shared the lawn mowing saga with our daughter who was away at college she asked me why I wasn't as hard on Sammy as I had been on her regarding the lawn mowing years earlier.

I explained to her that I had lowered my expectations. I mowed around the house and out beyond the landscape beds to the large, open section of lawn before turning the mower over to Sam. When I looked out the upstairs window and saw that bits and pieces of the lawn were mowed and bits and pieces of the lawn were not mowed I decided that it didn't really matter as long as all the trees were still standing when Sammy finished mowing.

I later figured out that the hum and motion of the mower made Sam too sleepy to safely mow so once again the lawn mowing responsibilities became mine and mine alone.

TRUTH: Standards change. If all the trees are standing when the lawn mowing is finished it is a good mow.

OREO

Butterscotch was a feisty, little brown gerbil. He amused himself by taunting the family cat, Pasha. If Butterscotch had been as clever as he was feisty he would not have exposed his tummy at the bars of the cage. The first time that Pasha scratched him he healed. The second scratch was deep and Butterscotch died.

Butterscotch was Sammy's pet. His cage was in Sammy's bedroom and Sammy was responsible for feeding him, making certain that he had water, and giving him a treat each evening. Although the "chirpy" little rodent would bite anyone any chance he got, Sammy liked Butterscotch. When I took Butterscotch to school and read *If You Give a Mouse a Cookie* all of the children were fascinated with Butterscotch.

Following the story Sammy and I told the children about gerbils. Sam explained that rodents' teeth grow so that they need to chew to wear down the growth. He also told them that a gerbil's life span is three to four years.

When Butterscotch died prematurely I was anxious about Sam's reaction. It was simple. Sam's body became rigid and he asked, "Can I get anudder one?" When I responded positively that he certainly could get another gerbil the grieving was over. It was simple: get another one.

Sam was in the fifth grade when Butterscotch died at the claw of Pasha. I told Sam that he could get another gerbil and that he would get another gerbil when we went to the city for his next doctor's appointment.

During our drive to the city Sammy played his Game Boy and said little. When we pulled into the parking lot at the pet store Sam asked if he could get any gerbil and I assured him that he could choose any gerbil that he wanted.

Once inside the store Sammy asked me several more times if he could have any gerbil and I repeatedly assured him that he could choose his new gerbil. Decision making caused anxiety for Sam. After looking at two pens crawling with gerbils Sam asked me if he could have the black and white gerbil. Again, I told Sammy that he could have any gerbil that he liked. I had never seen a black and white gerbil. I thought that all gerbils were brown but it made no difference to me which gerbil Sam brought home.

I asked the sales associate to hold the black and white gerbil for a few hours while we completed our business. During those few hours Sam asked me over and over if he should get the black and white gerbil and each time he asked I told him that he should get the black and white gerbil if that was the gerbil he wanted.

We returned to the pet store late afternoon and purchased the black and white gerbil. The little gerbil was placed in a small cardboard box that looked like a take out food container with air holes.

As we left the pet store we talked about names for Sammy's new gerbil. We listed several possible names and it didn't take long for us to decide on "Oreo". Oreo was a logical name for a black and white gerbil.

Sammy carried the little carton containing his new gerbil to the car and soon we were on our way home. As I merged onto the interstate Sammy asked me if I knew why he had chosen the black and white gerbil. When I asked Sam why he had chosen the black and white gerbil he replied,

"Because he was different and I think the other gerbils were picking on him."

Tears welled in my eyes and splashed down my cheeks. I was glad that the sun had set and the dusk hid my tears from Sam.

Through the years I had never told Sam that he was different. Some school personnel thought that I should tell Sammy that he had Asperger's Syndrome but when I asked a doctor's opinion the response was, "Sam doesn't have the mental ability to comprehend his handicap so it would be cruel to tell him." All I had ever told Sam was that he had allergies. He received injections twice a week for his allergies and he took medication three times a day.

TRUTH: Sam knew that he was different and he had been a victim.

A PENNY FOR YOUR THOUGHTS

When Sammy wasn't in perpetual motion he was sitting motionless staring off into space. It seemed to be all or none with him.

When I watched Sammy staring off into space I always wondered what he was thinking. What was going through his mind?

Frequently when I saw Sammy staring I would ask him, "What do you think?" He would always answer in a flat voice, "Pretty good." I didn't know what Sammy was thinking and he didn't know what I was asking. This went on for years.

One day I explained to Sammy what I was asking. I wanted to know what he was thinking about. Was he thinking about his pets? Was he thinking about a movie? *What* was he thinking?

From that day until this day when I ask Sam what he is thinking he replies in a flat voice, "I dunno."

TRUTH: The response is more appropriate but still doesn't answer the question. Since thinking is abstract he perhaps doesn't understand the question.

BLESSINGS

There was a time when I believed that I needed to move to a big city with Sammy so that we could access medical specialists and educational programming specifically for Asperger's Syndrome students.

After giving this careful consideration I realized that our family had much more in small town America than we would ever have in the big city.

Our small community knew us and the vast majority embraced us and felt our pain. They all knew Sammy so when he ran out into the street they slowed down and/or stopped because they knew that he wasn't going to get out of their way.

Although we have had to drive to see medical specialists we would have been driving in a city, too. The local health facility has been excellent for routine bumps and bruises. They went above and beyond the call of duty when allergy injections were implemented. Not many nurses can smile and be kind while being kicked, bitten, and head butted.

Our small school's elementary special education teacher along with several classroom teachers met the challenge and provided excellent educational programming for Sam. These teachers were advocates for both Sam and our family. Most teachers did their best while a few only tolerated him in their classrooms. The support staff at our school was incredible. I had read about the importance of school support staff but I had never really thought about how much impact they might have on a student. A friendly, "Good morning," by the bus driver; a "Hey, Sam, how's it going?" from the cook; a custodian asking, "So, what do you hear from Sabrina," a para professional who genuinely likes their job and your student, along with numerous greetings and initiated conversations make school a comfortable environment.

There isn't a more accepting or loving church than our little country church. We are *family*. We are all sons and daughters in God's Family and we genuinely care about one another. We have been fortunate to have an intelligent and patient Pastor who nurtured Sam through confirmation and continued to provide opportunities for Sam to be actively involved in the church.

Sabrina has been an advocate for Sam through the years and her school classmates and friends followed her example. I know that I will never receive the "Mother of the Year" award but Sabrina is most definitely the "Sister of the Year" every year!

Due to my physical limitations I have employed housekeepers since before Sam's birth. A couple of the housekeepers bonded with Sammy and were employed by our family for several years. These women were a gift from God. They not only cleaned our house but they helped out with Sam which gave me a break and sometimes they just listened. I am forever grateful for having these awesome women in my life.

Speaking of awesome, I have a network of girlfriends who have offered support through the years. Although they all had families of their own with their own busy schedules and challenges I always knew that they cared. Having a handicapped child kept me so busy and so exhausted that I didn't have the time or energy to be a friend for many years but I always knew that they were there for me. One friend in particular was my angel. She helped with Sam at all school events while Sabrina participated in extra curricular activities. She was always able to make positive comments about Sammy and she never judged him or me. It is sometimes said that friends are the family that we choose for ourselves. She was the sister that I never had.

My two older brothers (heavy on the older) have been **UNCLES** among uncles. Both of my very most favorite older brothers established unique relationships with Sammy so that Sammy looks forward to holiday and other family gatherings.

I have to confess that I was surprised and deeply touched that these brothers of mine could tolerate Sam's idiosyncracies and love him for who he is.

My oldest brother, Rico, got me a sister the day he married my very most favorite sister-in-law. She has been there for me through the years through thick and thin, with and without hair. She is a compassionate, kind, and positive woman who has been a fabulous aunt and Godmother to my children. Since Uncle Rico and Auntie Polly didn't have children Uncle Rico never had to grow up. In fact, Uncle Rico often confessed that just because he had to grow old didn't necessarily mean that he had to grow up. Thus, this big, old kid was a great play-mate for his nephews and niece. I don't think that there was a game that he wouldn't play but he particularly liked to play Monopoly, Yahtzee, and cards. He probably liked those games because he had a better chance of winning than when he played video games. Although I had taught my kids that games were for fun and that winning wasn't important Uncle Rico shared his philosophy regarding winning and losing: Show me a good loser and I'll show you a loser. Uncle Rico not only played games but he patiently built models with Sam. It was their special activity and year after year Uncle Rico would bring action figure models for he and Sam to assemble. When Sam and Harry were in their late teens they asked Uncle Rico to play video games one night after everyone else had gone to bed. The next day Harry told me that he and Sam had only wanted to play one game but Uncle Rico had them playing until 2:30a.m! I didn't say anything but I think that he was likely trying to play until he could win! Every holiday when Uncle Rico arrived we announced, "Let the games begin."

My other brother, Uncle Beefcake, as Sammy affectionate-ly calls him, is the Father of my very most favorite nephew who is eighteen months older than Sam. Cousin Harry and Sam have grown up together and share a special bond. Harry has been a quality role model and genuine friend. Harry accepted Sammy for who he was. When Sam would lose control I would often hear Harry say, "Sam, calm down." I always credited Harry's acceptance of Sam to his father.

For many years medical and educational specialists told me that I needed respite care but I was always too exhausted to negotiate the process of securing the service. With the help of an advocacy agency I was finally able to obtain respite care which gives me a weekly break. While I was only looking for a break I was delighted when both respite providers were intelligent, kind, enthusiastic, energetic individuals who bonded with Sam. They are people with many gifts who in turn see Sam's gifts.

The above mentioned people have been gifts in my life.

TRUTH: I am blessed.

WHAT UP WHERE?

Twice a year Sam saw a psychiatrist, Dr. Shrink. This doctor was mainly the medicine man since he really didn't do any counseling. If we needed help we could call any time but every six months was good enough for medications. (It wasn't long after we started looking for help that I decided that there is a reason why people become psychologists and psychiatrists but that's another book.)

Dick, Cousin Harry, Sam, and I were vacation bound but only after a stop for the summer appointment with Dr. Shrink. During elementary school when we visited Dr. Shrink I would usually talk with Dr. Shrink alone and then Sam would be invited to join us. This day was no exception other than the fact that Dick and Harry were with us. Dick sat outside reading the newspaper while Harry and Sam waited patiently as I talked with Dr. Shrink.

When Sam joined Dr. Shrink and me he was upset about something and talking and talking and talking but I couldn't understand what he was saying except the word, "ass," came through loud and clear every once in a while. The Dr. Shrink, Sam, and me part of the appointment was a bit of a waste of time since Sam was stuck on whatever he was babbling about. Dr. Shrink gave us new prescriptions and we were on our way.

We picked up Harry in the check in area and left. We joined Dick at the vehicle and headed west for a few days' vacation.

Sam had never quit talking about whatever he was stuck on so when we got in the vehicle I started asking questions. Between Sam and Harry I was made to understand that while Sam and Harry waited patiently for me while I talked with Dr. Shrink Sam had been the victim of an impatient employee.

Sam nearly always had a hand held game of some type in

his hands—the only exception being when he was at school. Today was no exception. He had a GigaPet which was a chatty, little toy that kept Sam amused. Well, it seems that one of the office employees found Sam's GigaPet a bit annoying and she took it upon herself to tell Sam that if he didn't "shut that thing off she would stick it up his ass".

Good grief! Can you imagine a clinic employee saying that to any client let alone an employee at a psychiatric clinic saying that to a client? I couldn't believe it and I wasn't allowed to forget it.

For the remainder of our vacation in and out of the car Sam was stuck on the GigaPet being up his butt. How would she get the GigaPet in his butt? How would the GigaPet feel in his butt? How would he get the GigaPet out of his butt? Dick and Harry found this rather amusing but since I was the one fielding the questions (over and over and over) I soon failed to see any humor in the discussions.

TRUTH: If I can listen to it twenty-four/seven surely you can tolerate it for ten minutes.

Six months later when we visited Dr. Shrink the first thing Sam told him was about the GigaPet being put up his butt. Since Dr. Shrink had difficulty understanding Sam I elaborated on the GigaPet and the clinic employee along with the effect it had on our vacation. Dr. Shrink was not at all pleased and he apologized profusely for any harm that may have resulted from this employee's inappropriate comments. Since Sam never forgets anything he still talks about the GigaPet up his butt from time to time.

BELONGING

During the twelve years before seventh grade Sam had been an outsider. If he had been a car he would have always been parked in perimeter parking.

Transitioning from sixth grade to seventh grade caused me great anxiety. Sam had talked about suicide many times during his elementary school years. He had talked about it several times during the summer between sixth and seventh grades.

Seventh grade meant a different special education teacher and a different resource room. Seventh grade meant a different teacher and room for each and every class. Seventh grade would definitely require a coordinator if Sam was going to get to classes on time and keep track of assignments. Lack of organizational skills was one of Sam's many deficits and one that would definitely make seventh grade a challenge.

Shortly after school started Sam told me that he was going to try out for the school play. I was not only surprised but a little apprehensive since I knew that the drama coach was a perfectionist. I didn't discourage Sam from trying out but I must admit that I didn't encourage him, either.

I went to try-outs with Sam so that I would know what was going on and so that I could scribe for Sam if necessary. When it was Sam's turn to read from a script Sam needed some help with some of the words. The students on stage with Sam were helpful and kind.

At the end of try-outs the drama coach, Mr. Wind, thanked all of the students for their interest. He told them that he knew that there weren't parts for everyone but that he wanted them to keep trying out for future productions. He told the students that try-out results would be posted outside his classroom door within the next few days. He was so positive and encouraging to the students.

I was more than a little surprised when Sam ecstatically

announced that he had a part in the fall play. He had one line in the first act of the play. He had a part.

Little did I realize just what this one line in the first act of the fall play would mean to Sam. There were several junior and senior girls that took Sam under their wings. They mentored Sammy and kept him out of trouble during rehearsals. During the school day it was the drama kids who smiled at Sam and greeted him in the halls. It took Sam no time at all to develop a deep respect and strong admiration for Mr. Wind. Sam had one line in the first act but he really had so much more. He had a part in the fall play but bigger than that, he had a part in the drama program. He belonged. After all these years of being an outcast he finally belonged and it made all the difference.

During parent teacher conferences I visited with Mr. Wind whom I had known for years. When I thanked him for giving Sammy a chance he told me that he enjoyed working with Sam. He told me that Sam was easy to work with because he was eager to please and had no attitude .

Since moving into the community years earlier I had observed the success of the drama program. I had seen many, many students flourish under the direction of Mr. Wind. Drama students presented themselves well and seemed to exude self confidence. I knew that Mr. Wind had made a difference in the lives of many, many students throughout his teaching/coaching career but I truly believed that he had made more of a difference in Sam's life than all the previous students' lives combined. I realized that I had known Mr. Wind for years but I hadn't really known him and I was amazed and delighted to see the drama coach side of him. He loved his work and he loved his students and they knew it.

TRUTH: Belonging makes all the difference in the world. No one can be all things to all people but we all have the ability to make a difference for someone.

"WAKEY, WAKEY..."

Dick strongly encouraged Sam to go out for football as a seventh grader. So, fall of seventh grade found Sam and me looking for football gear—foot attire, lightweight undergarments for warmth, and other undergarments that I had never seen before. I also learned how to disassemble a football uniform, launder the uniform, and reassemble the pieces. It was quite a feat for me.

Not only did I purchase the football gear, I shuttled Sam between football practices and games and play practice. He was a busy young man and I was a busy Mom but I was thrilled that Sam was involved in extra-curricular activities.

I purposely arrived early to pick Sam up from practices so that I could watch. I watched the team run drills with Sam coming in last. I watched the team end practice by running laps with Sammy coming in dead last. Since running was difficult to impossible for Sam given his inability to coordinate his body he really was "dead" last because he was exhausted.

As difficult as practices were for Sam he had a coach that encouraged him. The coach nicknamed Sam "Big Dog" and Sam worked hard to live up to his nickname. Sam was a big boy but he was just as clumsy as he was big. So, it came as no surprise to me when he was sidelined with an injury to his Achilles tendon.

In addition to the uniform and necessary undergarments, being last in drills and exercises, shuttling Sam from out of town games back to school for drama practice, "Big Dog", and the injury, I vividly recall an incident at an out of town game.

Sam didn't know what time his team played. Given my love of the game it was no wonder that finding the football field was a major feat for me. This was back when I thought that I was running for "Mother of the Year" so I was front and center in the bleachers before the team was on the field.

I understood nothing about the game except that the team scored when the ball was taken over the line at the end of the field. Very few if any parents knew about my ignorance or lack of exuberance for the game. I took my cues from the parents around me and cheered at what seemed to be appropriate times.

During this particular game Sam either tackled or just plain ran into an opponent knocking him to the ground. From across the field I saw Sam bend over the player and place his hands on the face guard of his helmet. It wasn't long and a referee was in Sam's face. After the game Sam asked me what "taunting" meant. When I asked him how the word was used he told me that the referee had told him that he couldn't taunt or he would receive a penalty. Sam had shaken the helmet of his opponent while he was on the ground and said, "Wakey, wakey, eggs and bakey!" So, that was taunting.

The following year when I picked Sam up from summer camp I was prepared to stop at an athletic store and purchase him new football spikes for his eighth grade season. Sam seemed a little hesitant about purchasing spikes and as we talked Sam said that he wasn't sure that he wanted to play football. My first thought was, "How will I explain this to his father?"

Sam told me that he felt rushed when he needed to go from a football game right to drama practice. Since Sam had only two speeds (slow and slower) I knew that this was difficult for him and caused stress. I suggested that we make lists of all the things that Sam liked about football and all the things that Sam liked about drama. After listing all the things that he liked we would make lists of all the things that Sam didn't like about football and all the things that Sam didn't like about drama. This might help Sam make his decision regarding football participation.

For over two hours of our travels we talked about football and drama. After making the afore mentioned lists Sam decided to participate in drama and not to participate in football. When I asked Sam what he liked best about drama he answered, "Everybody works togedder".

Working together is definitely a life skill and I believed that Sam had made a good choice. Given the lengthy conversation prior to Sam's decision making I was not the least bit concerned about Dick's response to Sam's choice. Sam knew what felt good to him and he had expressed himself brilliantly.

TRUTH: Despite handicaps, children know what feels good and what doesn't.

PICKING

Along with ADHD, TS, multiplex-developmental disorder, sensory dysfunction, autism, asperger's syndrome, and bi-polar symptoms Sam was also diagnosed with OCD—obsessive compulsive disorder.

Sam was a picker. He picked his nose, sometimes until it bled; he picked his finger and toe nails and the skin around the nails, sometimes until they bled; he picked clothing, sometimes until it was totally shredded; he picked holes in upholstered furniture; and he picked wallpaper right off the wall.

As much as I tried to put an end to the picking I was never successful. When I noticed a correlation between stress and picking I could reduce the picking by reducing Sam's level of stress. I also noticed that anything abrasive got picked so I removed all tags from clothing.

Following my realization of the relationship between stress and picking I felt like I became a detective. When Sam was pick, pick, picking I tried to find the source of his stress so that I could reduce or eliminate it, thus, reducing or eliminating the picking.

The peak of Sam's picking came the fall of seventh grade. For several weeks he destroyed two to three pair of underwear a day along with socks and numerous shirts. I found piles of threads and elastic pieces behind the sofa where he watched TV and under his bed. During this time I purchased new underwear and socks weekly when I traveled to purchased groceries.

I listened to and watched Sam after school everyday. I went to school to talk with teachers. At Sam's IEP meeting I talked about Sam's picking and stress and it seemed to fall on deaf ears. I looked at those in attendance. Some had their heads down in a resting position, some were looking at their watches eager for the meeting to be over, while others were just preoccupied with their own agendas. When I removed a zip-loc bag from my brief case and dumped a large pile of threads and elastic bits and pieces onto the table they became interested. A visual aid was all it took to gain their assistance in reducing Sam's stress. The team agreed to modify and reduce assignments and eliminate homework. When the workload was decreased so was the stress and consequently the picking became minimal.

Another mystery solved.

TRUTH: If advocating for your child requires you to be a detective than you must become a detective. Your child needs you.

DO, RE, MI, FA, SO, LA, TI, DO

Fifth graders get instruments, take lessons, and start playing in the elementary band. Two years of piano lessons was a prerequisite to playing a band instrument but this rule was waived for Sam according to his IEP.

Sam wanted to play an instrument. He wanted to play in the band. After talking with the band teacher it was decided that Sam would play drums.

Sam and I went to the music store in a nearby city and purchased drum sticks and a drum pad for practicing. Everyday Sam practiced. He was required to document his practice time and he kept his time sheet by his drum pad and sticks and kept track of his minutes of practice.

During the two music concerts that year I noticed that Sam struck the snare drum with his sticks but he didn't do any rolling.

The next year there was a new band teacher. Sam was moved to the bass drum. At the first concert I noticed the director specifically motioning to Sam when he should strike the drum. I talked with the special education teacher about this and was told that a para-professional had been working with Sam but he wasn't getting a feel for the music. Sam couldn't feel the beat.

The new band teacher was professional and demanding of his students. Some students that were too lazy to practice quit band so Sam thought that the popular thing to do was quit band. I would not allow Sam to quit band. I told him that he chose to participate in band and that he was not a quitter.

As I watched the band perform the following year it occurred to me that the band teacher was directing each and every bass drum action along with directing the entire band. I knew that it wouldn't be long until Sam's peers would be impatient with him because he just wasn't able to hold the beat for the band.

Since I had told Sam that he couldn't quit band I needed to think of another strategy. I talked with both the band teacher and the special education teacher. I thanked the band teacher for being patient with Sam. I told him that he had been more than fair to Sam. I told him that Sam's schedule for the following year would conflict with band so that he would need to find another bass drum player.

I told Sam that he would not be playing in the band the following year. I thought that Sam would be happy but no, he was oppositional. He wanted to play in the band. He was the bass drum player and the band needed him. I explained to Sam that he had been in band for several years but that his class schedule for next year had a conflict with band. I told Sam that he had done his part and now it was time for someone else to do their part. Sam thought a couple minutes and then said, "Well, Mr. Thomasson lost the best drummer he ever had."

TRUTH: Ringo he wasn't.

During parent teacher conferences that fall I relayed to Mr.

Thommason Sam's comment about losing the best drummer he ever had. Mr. Thommason just smiled. I had great respect for Mr. Thommason when he came to town and gave band members a list of expectations. I respected Mr. Thommason when he wore a tuxedo to each and every band concert and conducted himself professionally. I respected him even more for patiently working with my son. I can't imagine being a professional musician trying to direct a band with a bass drummer who can't feel the beat or hold a tempo. He had gone above and beyond and I will be forever grateful.

LOGICAL

Sabrina and Dick were hunters. Sam had been shooting a BB gun and .22 at summer camp and had received awards for marksmanship.

Sam anxiously awaited his twelfth birthday, taking gun training, and deer hunting in November. I registered Sam for gun training and spoke with the instructor about Sam's special needs and accommodations. I read the manual to Sam before each class and again after class. Sam and I reviewed the manual prior to the final exam and Sam passed the test. He was ecstatic and I was happy for him. Sam had passed the gun safety test with his peers. For someone who didn't have much experience with success this was an event to be celebrated.

Dick and Sam went to a gun dealer and purchased a 275 Winchester short mag. Sam was thrilled with his new rifle and he could hardly wait for deer season. Dick and Sam sighted in the new rifle and Sam and I laid out blaze orange clothing for opening day.

Sam sat in his deer stand each evening waiting for a buck. It was early in the season when I received *the* phone call. Sam had shot a buck and I needed to come with the camera. I was so excited that I couldn't find the camera fast enough. I grabbed my blaze orange jacket and cap and drove to the hunting cabin where I found Sam, Dick, and the eight point buck. I took many, many pictures. I kept waiting for Sam to "spill" the story of his first deer but he didn't. When I kept asking questions Sam simply said, "Mom, I took the class, I got a gun, I got a license, and I shot a deer."

It was simple. It was logical. It was concrete.

Sam was more excited about winning the big buck contest in the junior high division at school than he was about actually shooting the deer.

TRUTH: Concrete, logical sequencing makes the world predictable and understandable.

Sam has hunted every deer season since that first season when he was twelve years old. He has shot several bucks and has won three big buck contests. After several seasons of deer hunting Sam confided in me that he liked being at the hunting shack and playing cards and watching football and hanging out as much as he liked hunting. Being social is not typical of autism but Sam is social. Like one presenter said years ago, "If you know one autistic, you know one autistic."

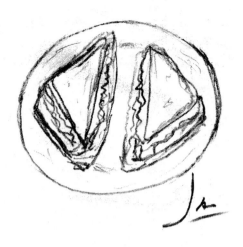

PEANUT BUTTER AND NO JELLY

Although I don't really remember when, there was point when Sam's educational focus changed from academics to life skills.

I had been reading and attending conferences to learn teaching strategies. I had picture cards and velcro strips to make visuals of morning and evening grooming routines. I made a list of laundry procedures. I had picture recipes.

Laundry and cooking were the life skills that we were targeting. I posted a large picture recipe of a peanut butter and jelly sandwich on a cupboard door in the kitchen.

When Sam saw the picture he indignantly asked, "Do you think that I'm dumb or what? I don't need a picture to make a sandwich." I took the picture recipe down and Sam made his sandwich. He poured a glass of milk and sat down to eat. After the first bite he looked at me and said, "No jelly."

Sam got up from the table and put some jelly on his sandwich. I got up from the table and placed the peanut butter and jelly picture recipe back on the cupboard door. No verbal exchange was required. We both understood.

TRUTH: Tasks requiring multiple steps require supports such as visual aids or written check off lists to ensure success.

DYSGRAPHIA

For years teachers attempted to teach Sam to print. It didn't seem to matter who was doing the teaching or what method or technique was used, Sam's printing was crude, nearly illegible, and unique to Sam.

Printing was difficult but cursive writing was impossible. Sam couldn't write or read cursive. Due to Sam's inability to print legibly or write in cursive it was determined that he was dysgraphic meaning that he was unable to communicate with written language.

Not only could Sam not make the physical letters basic to language communication, we found that grammar was like a foreign language to Sam.

It was about this time that specialists decided that enough time had been spent teaching skills that Sam couldn't learn. Sam was dysgraphic and there was a possibility that he had dyscalculia which meant that he was unable to do math.

From middle elementary school Sam's IEPs (individual educational plan) compensated for his inability to write in a variety of ways. Teachers were to make copies of their notes, students were to share notes with Sam, a para was to take notes for Sam, a para was to scribe for Sam, and a co-writer word processing program was to be used. When this was all delineated in Sam's IEP I often wondered why there were so many papers in his backpack with his chicken scratchings but if Sam wasn't complaining I wasn't asking.

After years of being diagnosed with dysgraphia accompanied by years of accommodations for the disability I was more than a little surprised when Sam was given a state standardized writing test. When the test results were back the students that had failed were called to the principal's office via an all school intercom. Sam was embarrassed and humiliated from being called to the principal's office to be notified of his failing. When he told me I wondered to myself, "How many times and in how many ways does the school need to tell my son that he is a failure? I work long and hard to build self-esteem and in a few thoughtless acts my efforts are null and void."

At Sam's next IEP meeting I inquired about the writing test being given to a dysgraphic student and I was told that the state required one test for a baseline score and it wouldn't be given again. I requested in writing that Sam not be given any more writing tests.

The following year without my knowledge Sam was given the state standardized writing test. Sam was wild that he had failed the test because he thought that he had done well. When I inquired about Sam being given the test again I was told that it was required by the state.

I acknowledge that I am not the sharpest pencil in the box but I do find it impossible to understand why a student with a dysgraphic diagnosis would be given a state standardized writing test. Would a blind student be given a visual reading test? Would a quadriplegic be required to run in the spring track and field competition?

I was upset until I received Sam's test results and then I was furious. After years and years with a dysgraphic diagnosis Sam was given a state standardized writing test. Following the test Sam was told that he failed and I was sent test results. Sam had scored in the first percentile. That means that if one hundred peers were tested in the state ninety-nine of them would have scored higher than Sam. I did *not* have a need to know this. Sam did not need to be told that he had failed again.

When I tried to pursue this at a local level I was given the smoke screen about being required by the state so I called the state office of education and made some inquiries. I was told that my son did not need to be tested. This went back and forth and back and forth with the local being large and in charge until I requested regional intervention along with an impartial mediator.

Guess what? Dysgraphic students do not need to take a state standardized writing test. DUH……

TRUTH: Do not assume that your child's best interests are first and foremost in any system including the educational and medical systems. Systems are flawed because people are flawed and when one assumes this is often what happens: ass/u/me

FAIR

Initially I was told that Sam couldn't participate in the pre-school Head Start program because it wouldn't be fair. Our family didn't meet the income criteria. When I asked the Head Start employee that gave me this news about her educational background she proudly told me that she had a two year degree in early childhood and six years' babysitting experience.

When Sammy started kindergarten there were two sections. Section 1 met Mondays and Wednesdays and every other Friday. Section 2 met Tuesdays and Thursdays and every other Friday. Since Sam was developmentally delayed and he seemed to learn best from repetition it was decided that Sam would attend kindergarten every day. Some people didn't think that it was fair that Sam went to kindergarten everyday while they had to pay daycare the days that their child wasn't in school.

During elementary school there were accommodations made for Sam. He used a "special" pencil that was weighted. He wore a weighted vest. He received assistance for some assignments in a resource room from a special education teacher. A para-professional or special education teacher read tests to Sam. A para-professtional scribed for Sam. Peers would tell Sam that his special treatment wasn't fair and that he was cheating.

Accommodations continued in junior high school and high school. Sam was able to take some courses twice. Peers told Sam that this wasn't fair.

My reaction to this talk about being fair was quite simple. Life is not fair and don't we know it!

TRUTH: Fair means that everybody gets what everybody needs.

NICE VS. SMART

Around the time the school was giving Sam state standardized tests and calling him to the principal's office via all call intercom to notify him of his failure Sam started telling me that he was dumb. Sam told me that he sucked at math, he couldn't write, and he failed all the tests.

While I listened to Sam I felt like everything I had worked so hard to establish had been erased. I had tried to be positive with Sammy by pointing out things that he did well. I complimented him when he did something well or did something kind for someone. I always thanked him when he did something for me or when he did his chores.

Sam had so many wonderful qualities. He was kind and generous and he had developed a fun sense of humor. Sam knew right from wrong. When Sam understood what was expected of him he worked hard to meet those expectations. Sam was my very most favorite son and I wanted him to feel needed and special. I wanted him to feel good about himself.

After listening to Sam berate himself I finally interrupted him to tell him about the many things that he did well. I told him that he was a nice person. I told him that the world had enough smart people. I told him that the world needed more nice people. Then I asked Sam if he had to choose to be with someone that was really smart or someone that was really nice who would he choose? Sam chose to be with the really nice person and that was exactly my point.

Nice people are always in demand. Nice people with good manners are in even greater demand.

In spite of Sam's failings at school Sam will succeed in life because being nice is a life skill.

TRUTH: It's nice to be important but it's more important to be nice.

OUCH!

During the years that Sabrina wore braces it became obvious that Sam's teeth were less than perfect. He had a severe under-bite and his front teeth protruded giving his peers inspiration to call him, "buck tooth".

Sam's general dentist recommended an orthodontic consult to rule out TMJ (temporal mandibular joint) issues. At this point in time I was not the least bit concerned about aesthetics but I knew that we didn't need any more problems so I made an appointment for Sam to be seen by the orthodontist that Sabrina was seeing.

Dr. Bracket was an older, well respected and well established orthodontist. I was impressed with the consultation process when Sabrina started wearing braces. I particularly liked the fact that he made the braces and their maintenance the responsibility of the wearer. I also liked the efficiency with which his office was run. All those things combined with Sabrina's end results of straight and beautiful teeth and a model perfect smile made him a guru in orthodontia in my opinion.

I met with Dr. Bracket before he examined Sam. I told him that Sam had Asperger's Syndrome and allergies and what that might mean for braces maintenance. I explained that I wasn't as concerned with aesthetics as I was concerned for long term jaw maneuverability.

Dr. Bracket met Sam and examined his mouth and face. He took impressions and made a model jaw for consultation purposes.

At the following appointment Dr. Bracket showed Sam and me the model jaw and explained what was going on in Sam's mouth. Correcting the underbite would require surgery. Braces would be applied only if we agreed to surgery because braces alone couldn't rectify the situation. After a lengthy explanation ending with the cost of the braces and surgery Dr. Bracket looked at me and asked, "Are you sure you want to spend that kind of money on this kid?"

I couldn't believe what I had heard. I was so offended by Dr. Bracket's callous and cruel question. I felt like someone had punched me in the stomach and I could barely breathe. I could feel tears welling in my eyes. I wasn't just offended. I was hurt and angry. What could this man possibly be thinking? This was my son. Why would I not want to ensure good oral health for my son? Although Sam had heard Dr. Bracket's question it seemed to have no effect on him. I, on the other hand, was growing more furious by the second.

As we left Dr. Bracket's office I made up my mind that if we did indeed choose to spend that kind of money on this kid it would be with a different orthodontist.

TRUTH: Education does not guarantee a lack of ignorance. Compassion and "bedside manner" aren't automatically granted with a medical degree.

OH, DO YOU KNOW
THE MUFFIN MAN?

Sam bolted through the door ranting and raving. I couldn't understand what he was upset about so I put an after school snack on the table and sat down with him.

When Sam had calmed down he told me that he thought that I would be receiving a call from the school because he had busted a kid's glasses. When I asked him how the glasses got broken this is what he told me:

Sam had been sitting at a breakfast table at school with his peers when the kid sitting next to him put his muffin down the back of Sam's shirt and then used his hand against the back of Sam's shirt to mash it in. Sam put his hand on the back of the perpetrator's head and with all his might slammed the kid's face to the table. And, that's what broke the glasses. Sam eats breakfast at home before getting on the bus so I don't know why he was at the breakfast table but he evidently was eating a second breakfast.

I could tell that Sam was anxious. He likely thought that I was going to scold him or take away privileges. I didn't.

I reminded Sam of elementary school when I had finally had enough bullying and I gave him permission to hit back; to defend himself. I told Sam that if the kid hadn't put the muffin down his shirt that he wouldn't have slammed his head to the table and the glasses wouldn't have gotten broken. I told Sam that it was the owner of the glasses that was at fault and that if the school called I would tell them just that.

While Sam ate his snack I thought about the muffin incident. Why were kids so cruel?

It wasn't long and a thought sparked a smile. I asked Sam if he knew the Muffin Man song. When he told me that he didn't I sang it for him and we both laughed and laughed. I gave Sam permission to sing the song at breakfast the following day.

The school never did call me regarding the muffin incident and it soon became history.

Sometime after that incident Sam was complaining about a teacher's yelling. Since I knew the teacher I found it nearly impossible to believe. In fact, I told Sam that he was sensitive to volume. I told him that he was misinterpreting the teacher's intentions. After several years of Sam's complaints I went to school for a little "Come to Jesus meetin'," which resulted in Sam having permission to leave the classroom when he felt afraid as a result of the yelling.

TRUTH: Pushed far enough into a corner, animals as well as people will come out fighting. Enough is enough.

NEVER

During a six month block of time I met four parents from four different families with autistic children. Looking back on these parents I marvel that we ever connected because there was so much *chance* involved. Or was there?

A mutual acquaintance told a young father with a recently diagnosed son about me. When he called he sounded so timid, tired, and terrified. He and his young wife had a newly diagnosed autistic four year old son and twin baby girls. We talked for a very long time and I have never forgotten him or his family. Before hanging up the phone I made a point of telling him that eighty percent of marriages with handicapped children end in divorce. I cautioned him to take care of his wife and their relationship. I couldn't sleep that night thinking about them because I knew some of the things that they would likely experience and I hurt for them. Somehow I wanted to "fix it" for them but I knew that I couldn't.

When a middle aged businessman called on us I was shocked to learn that he had a forty year old autistic daughter in an institution. It wasn't until he was ready to leave and we were looking at our aquarium and talking about the calming effects of aquariums that the man felt safe enough to share an inner hurt with us. My son was less than half the age of his daughter. I couldn't help but think of the great strides that have been made in understanding autism. When he told us about the need to remove his daughter from their home to protect their other children and about being judged by the public for this action I could feel his pain and I wondered who would judge the judges.

Then there was the salesperson in the boutique who had just institutionalized her seven year old son. I could see the freshness and depth of her pain as tears welled in her eyes.

She was feeling encouraged because her son was already

experiencing some success in sleep management and toilet training as a result of the institution's twenty-four/seven behavior management program. I felt so blessed because I was able to have my son at home and I could honestly enjoy him for the unique individual that he is.

Lastly there was the survey taker who had a seven year old autistic son. She reminded me of the mother that I had been years earlier—so worried about how this whole autistic thing would play out and so terrified of the consequences of having a handicapped sibling for her "normal" child.

With each of the above parents I felt an instant and lasting bond. Each and every one of them had experienced the pain of watching their child be rejected by peers. Not being invited to birthday parties and being chosen last along with never meeting the milestone markers of "normal" growth and development doesn't seem to hurt the child nearly as much as it devastates the parent. Although the pain changes it never goes away. **Never, no, not ever.**

I couldn't impress on these parents enough that they are *not* the lone ranger. Although they perhaps feel like the lone *stranger* they really are not alone. Families had handicapped children before their child was born and sad, but true, parents will continue to have handicapped children. As trite as it may sound: united we stand; divided we fall.

TRUTH: If we can't lighten someone else's load we really have no purpose. Since we are the "experts" on our handicapped children we need to learn from each other and support one another.

FUN

Being in the survival mode year after year left no time for photo albums and/or scrapbooks. Sam's babybook had one entry.

When I realized that Sam's high school graduation was within his grasp it dawned on me that after not completing Sabrina's photo album for her high graduation I had promised myself that I would complete Sam's photo album/scrapbook so that it could be displayed at his graduation open house. (I was still of the opinion that the school administration and some teachers would be hosting a celebration party for Sam's graduation since it would be Sam's as well as my exit from their radar screens.) Nevertheless, I had set this goal and from some previous experiences I knew that I couldn't count on the school.

I went to the basement room which is known as "Santa's Workshop" where I have nearly thirty years of photos in piles and shoe boxes. Can you even begin to visualize that? Since I was a Mom on a mission I was not to be overwhelmed by what seemed to be "mission impossible".

First off, I set up a system. It seemed to me that it would be a great idea to sort the photos chronologically. This worked well except for the years and years and years of photos taken before cameras had photo dating abilities. Not to be thwarted I leaned forward sorting by hair style, height, number of teeth missing, clothing, and absolutely anything that gave a clue to the vintage of the photo.

Although there was an urgency to complete this daunting task I found myself in a non-productive state time and time and time again. There were notes that Sam and Sabrina had written to me. Naturally, I had to read them and savor the moment. I traveled back in time so to speak and enjoyed times that I couldn't enjoy at the time because I was so sleep deprived. The photos were incredible. We had been there and done that and we were all so happy—lots and lots of smiley faces. Since our family celebrates everything we had pictures and pictures and pictures of extended family with smiley faces. There were photos of tiny babies, baptisms, first teeth, first steps, first days of school (each and every grade), birthday parties, family vacations, Christmases, Easters, Fourth of Julys, Halloweens, sporting events, horseback riding, with pets, hunting, and so much more. Looking at these photos reminded me why I often jokingly referred to our ranch as The Funny Farm. As I perused the boxes and piles of photos it stirred up emotions as well as so many, many memories of fun times.

In spite of ourselves, we had had fun.

TRUTH: Our family put the FUN in dysfunctional and as my brother always says, "Who has more fun than a pack of buffoons?"

HAPPY VALENTINE'S DAY, SON

The valentine read, "When you were a little boy we changed you eight to ten times a day." Open the card and it read, "Now we wouldn't change anything about you. Happy Valentine's Day, Son."

That was the valentine that I mailed to my very most favorite son when he was sixteen years old.

When I read the card I instantly knew that it was *the* card for Sammy. The card said everything that I had been feeling and believing but not putting together into words.

Our son was sixteen years old and all grown up. He was looking ahead to his junior and senior years and then the real world.

Through all those survival years Sammy had grown into a wonderful, one of a kind, guy. At sixteen years of age Sammy had a warm and loving spiritual side. He was kind, polite, and well mannered. He was honest and he knew right from wrong. He had an incredibly zany sense of humor accompanied with an infectious laugh. Sam wasn't perfect but I didn't know another sixteen year old boy that I liked better. I didn't know another sixteen year old boy that I thought would make a greater contribution to society.

Happiness had always been my goal for Sam. Every meeting that I attended began with goal setting and I always said that my goal for Sam was for him to be happy. It was a simple goal but years ago it seemed so unattainable. Now, at age sixteen, Sam was happy and he possessed personal qualities that would pave the way for a lifetime of happiness.

"Now we wouldn't change anything about you. Happy Valentine's Day, Son." I added: Continue to grow in grace, Sam, and have a happy life.

TRUTH: Love isn't just for Valentine's Day. I love Sam forever and always.

BUSTED

I love my son dearly but he was not a lovable child. When Sammy was a young boy he was totally out of control. He kicked, screamed, head butted, and bit. He rarely slept and when he did it was erratic—no rhyme nor reason to his wake and sleep times. He was developmentally delayed so he was barely verbal and what he did say was difficult to understand. He stood on his head, rolled, and curled into a human ball. His eyes and nose ran and he coughed and coughed. He picked the skin from his fingers until they bled. He picked his nose until it bled. He picked wallpaper off the walls. He picked holes in his clothing and upholstered furniture. He was a finicky eater and smelled everything before deciding whether or not he would put it into his mouth.

I knew that there was something "wrong" with my child but I didn't know what *it* was.

I read whenever I could but Sammy was a very time consuming young man. So, while I read and prayed and attempted to make sense of my son I protected him from himself and his surroundings. I calmed him when he was anxious and I loved him.

During the early years I dreaded holidays. Christmas and the Fourth of July were times when family could see that Sam was late for each and every developmental milestone. Even though a doctor had told us that Sammy would function best in his home environment with no changes I insisted that we celebrate holidays with family—either at our home or theirs. I thought that Sam could be desensitized to change. However, Sam continued to tantrum and stand on his head and not eat what was served.

One day when we were at my parents' home my dad told me that I had waited so long for a baby that I had spoiled him. He went on to tell me that Sam had me wrapped around his little finger and that he manipulated me. My mother had already told me that I should "get to the seat of the problem".

My mother's advice didn't bother me because she had spanked me and my brothers when we were kids but I will never forget my dad's comment. My dad is most likely the nicest, kindest, most gentle man on the face of the earth. He is a loving, spirit filled man. I was devastated by his comment. I felt that my parenting skills were definitely lacking and I thought that my dad believed Sammy to be devious. How could my dad, the man that I loved and respected my entire life, be so disapproving of me and my son?

Years went by and Sam received various diagnoses but the diagnoses didn't come with cures so he continued to not conform to the expectations of my mother and father. They had two perfect grandchildren and they had Sam.

As my parents aged they became less inhibited in expressing their disapproval of Sam. Christmases became nearly unbearable for me. My parents stay with my family for two to three weeks during Christmas and during that time my mother challenges everything that Sam says. It seems that both of my parents glare at Sam every time he opens his mouth. Ironically, Sammy doesn't have a clue. He loves his grandparents and waits for their visits. He loves to play cards with them. He has not picked up on their disapproval.

At one time I severed communication with my mother for about a month. She accused Sam of taking something from her house. (as in stealing) While Sam slept I searched the pockets of the jeans that he had been wearing, his backpack, his room and the car. When I called to tell her that Sam didn't have the missing object she didn't back down. She told me that Sam was the last person in the room before the object disappeared. It was cut and dried. In her opinion, Sam was guilty.

Since Sam's birth I feel like I have been fighting the health care system and some of its doctors, insurance companies, the education system, the county, and the insensitive and judgemental public. I should not need to fight my family.

TRUTH: My give a damn is busted.

JOHN DEERE PANTS VS. LOW RISE FLARES

His waist was thirty inches and his inseam was thirty-two inches. When he descended the stairway with more difficulty than usual I looked to see what would come around the corner. When Sam appeared he had a grip on the waistband of the jeans he was wearing to keep them from falling down.

It was obvious to me that Sam was wearing Dick's John Deer Pants (44X32's) and as much as I wanted to laugh I knew better. Sam looked at me and asked, "What happened to my jeans?" Without even a hint of a smile I replied, "I think that I put your dad's jeans in your chest of drawers by mistake. Take them off and I'll put them where they belong."

Sam did just as I had instructed him to do and went back to his bedroom to get jeans. As I put Dick's jeans in his closet I thought about what had just happened. How could Sam have not known that the *big* jeans were not his? Did Sam think that his jeans had grown? Did Sam think that he had shrunk? Was Sam just plain not able to process what had just happened? I didn't know the answers to my questions and I knew that Sam didn't know the answers, either. In fact, I was pretty sure that he didn't even question what had just happened.

Some years later Sam came downstairs ready for school. While watching Sam walk toward the coat rack I didn't recognize the jeans that he was wearing. He kept tugging on the belt loops to hike them up but it didn't deter him. He grabbed his jacket and went out to the school bus.

When he returned home that day he was still tugging at his jeans. I didn't recognize the jeans but thought that maybe they were a new pair that we had set aside until he grew into them.

When I did laundry that week the ill-fitting jeans were in Sam's clothes basket. When I removed them from clothes dryer to fold them I noticed that they were a size 10! They were Sabrina's jeans! She had been home for a long week-end and left her jeans in the clothes hamper upstairs and they had gotten in with Sam's clothes. By this time Sam could take a little joke so I told him that he had been wearing Sabrina's jeans. Sam didn't act like he thought wearing Sabrina's jeans was funny so I knew better than to express my amusement.

After Christmas that year when Sam rushed downstairs and to the coat rack desperately trying to get to the school bus on time I recognized the ill-fitting jeans instantly and said, "Sam, you're wearing Sabrina's jeans again." He replied, "I don't have time to change. They're good enough." Low rise with flared legs made these jeans nothing short of stylish but to Sam they were *good enough*.

This time when I rescued Sabrina's jeans from Sam's laundry I mailed them to her. I wrote her a note telling her about the jeans fiascos but somehow I knew that she wouldn't see the humor of the situation like I did. Who could?

TRUTH: Sensory integration dysfunction coupled with a lack of executive functioning makes for *interesting* situations. Perhaps this partially demonstrates why Sam will always need a co-pilot.

SO LONG, GOOD-BYE...

My ongoing medical concerns started before Sabrina's birth so my health issues have been a way of life for our family.

One time when I told Sam that I needed to have surgery and that I would be gone for a few days he responded with, "Are you going to die?" I told Sam that I didn't think that I was going to die but that everyone died sometime. All living things die sometime. Sam quickly asked, "If you die can I have your car?" I told Sam that since he didn't have a driver's license he had no need for my vehicle. I went on to explain to Sam that such a question was inappropriate and hurtful. I told him that it would have been better for him to have said that he hoped that my surgery went well and that I would be feeling well soon.

Years later when my father was diagnosed with cancer I told Sammy that Grandpa had cancer. Sam asked, "Is PaPa going to die?" I told Sam that yes, PaPa was going to die. We didn't know when PaPa was going to die but he was going to die. Sam asked, "When Papa dies can I have his boat?" I explained that he couldn't have PaPa's boat and that it was rude and hurtful to ask such a question. I told Sam that it would be better for him to say that he felt sad that PaPa was going to die.

A short time later Dick was diagnosed with cancer. When Dick told Sam that he had cancer Sam asked, "If you die can I have your snowcat?" I patiently told Sam that he couldn't have his dad's snowcat. I explained that asking such a question was poor manners and hurtful. I told Sam that it would have been better to tell his dad that he was sorry about his cancer. I told him that it was okay to ask parents questions about surgeries and medical conditions but that we didn't plan to gain property from someone's death.

Reflecting on these three similar incidents I was reminded

of Sam's reaction to the death of his two gerbils and his teddy bear hamster and his dog. Each and every time a pet died Sam had immediately asked, "Can I get anudder one?"

Sam seemed to compartmentalize death. Healthy or not, Sam's method of dealing with death seemed to work for him but I always wondered what went on in Sam's head and heart regarding death.

TRUTH: Regardless of strategies or repetition of situations, I have never extinguished one undesirable behavior.

WANTED: ONE MOTHER

Soon after Sam's birth I began to worry about who would care for him and love him if I should die. Since my health has been tenuous it was a realistic concern. There were times when I know that I took care of myself just so that I could take care of Sam.

When Sabrina was young she looked out for Sam and protected him from the world around him whenever she could. Sometimes she expressed anger that Sam consumed so much of my time and energy and she was angry when she found out how expensive Sam was one day when she picked up prescriptions from the pharmacy. For the most part Sabrina was a loving and protective sister.

Once when we were traveling during the winter when Sam was a pre-schooler we stopped at a McDonald's for lunch. Sam went to the restroom and I monitored the time that he was gone closely because I was always afraid of abuse in public restrooms. Sam was vulnerable and public restrooms were ripe with opportunity for abuse. While I was keeping an eye on my watch I noticed Sabrina walk over to a table of young boys. She stooped over so that her face was level with theirs. As Sabrina was returning to our booth I saw the young boys get up, dispose of the remnants of their meals, and leave. I thought that this was a bit odd so I asked Sabrina about their exit. Sabrina said, "You know how Sammy walks with his snowboots? He kind of shuffles. Well, when Sam walked by their table on his way to the restroom they snickered at him. So, I went over and told them not to F with my brother."

I was stunned. I didn't know that my little girl was capable of using such a word and it was years before the onset of my copralalia. (Technical term for use of bad language—in my case it was an incredible method of stress release.) However shocked I was at Sabrina's language the shock was far superseded by my pride in her protective action. I knew that Sabrina would watch out for Sammy in the short term but who would take care of my baby in the long term?

For years this was an issue with me. I didn't know anyone who could or would love my impulsive and out of control child. Sam was so all consuming. He was my son and I think that God gave me a minimum of a double dose of maternal instinct because I loved Sam for who he was and I was fiercely protective of him. (Although I always told my children that if anyone abducted them that they would be returned in a hurry. I also told them that I knew why some species ate their young. Kidding aside, I loved my children—unconditionally—and I was proud of them.) By the time I was scheduling my sixth surgery Sabrina was in college. She firmly but lovingly let me know that I didn't need to worry about Sam. She could and would take care of him should anything happen to me. She may not be the caregiver but she would see to it that he was well cared for and that he would continue to live the lifestyle to which he was accustomed.

Since I had long since quit running for "Mother of the Year" the contest hardly entered my mind but I knew that I had been successful in parenting Sabrina. She was a competent, intelligent, compassionate young woman and she had definitely internalized the family value system that I had imparted.

No longer did I need to worry about who would take care of my son because I knew that Sabrina would take care of my son and her brother.

TRUTH: "Train up a child in the way he should go and when he is old he will not depart from it." Proverbs 22:6

Blood *is* thicker than water.

I GET IT, DO YOU GET IT?

Sitting in sunny Arizona writing and sewing and playing bridge and meeting new people has been a blessing that has allowed me physical and mental healing. I have been inspired and I have some new perspectives.

I get it and I want you to get it, too.

My grandmother was a quiet Christian woman whose life was devoted to serving her Lord and Savior. As a young woman her family starved out in North Dakota and moved to Minnesota where she would bury an infant son and her only daughter. When her husband died of pneumonia in his early forties she was left a young widow with two sons. I think that Grandma survived great adversity but I never heard her complain. She had two sons, two daughters-in-law and seven grandchildren and the love of the Lord and all she wanted was for her family to know the Lord as their personal savior. The older she got the more frequently she would ask me if I knew the Lord. Toward the end of her life she would repeat, "He will never leave me nor forsake me." She lived a life of faith looking forward to eternal life in heaven.

As a young girl I contemplated being a Pastor. That was before women clergy were common and my Pastor told me that there were many ways to share the message other than being a preacher. He mentioned Christian mothers, teachers, Sunday school teachers, Brownie and Girl Scout leaders, nurses, etc. This was before women's lib!

I became a teacher and I loved teaching. I believed that I could make a positive impact in the lives of my students and that they in turn would make a difference in the lives of their children. I lived in a community that had a church on every corner. The vast majority of my students came from Christian homes so when I taught values and choices I was hoping that my students would see that peer pressure was not an issue when choices were based on personal (Christian) values. Instead, I was accused of teaching secular humanism. Although I was a recent college graduate and I thought that I knew almost everything, I had never heard of secular humanism.

My teaching career was cut short due to health issues but I was able to continue to work part time coordinating an Early Childhood Family Education Program. I was a parent and I totally believed the philosophy that parents are a child's first and most important teachers. Empowering parents became my mission. This career came to an abrupt end not too long after Sam joined our family. It was difficult if not impossible to teach parenting when I was not a good role model. My own child was out of control so how could I possibly know anything about parenting?

My passion for teaching was not to be deterred. I taught Sunday School and I taught Vacation Bible School. There were years when I hired a babysitter to take care of Sam so that I could be involved with Vacation Bible School. I knew that there wasn't anything more important than teaching children that God loves them.

Through God's guidance and my love of teaching, my family brought three exchange students into our home. Yes, during the survival years I also parented three teen-aged exchange students. I was much younger then but my theory that God would never give me more than I could handle played out.

I didn't realize it then but when I couldn't handle it alone He sent angels and He continues to send me angels. I once heard a woman say, "Angels all around you," when she was leaving a loved one and I thought that it was so sweet. It is my hope and prayer for all of us that we be surrounded by angels who will protect us from harm and be constant reminders of God's love.

Although I watched very little television while in Arizona when I heard an advertisement for a Billy Graham ministries production it took me back in time to my childhood. I fondly remembered our telephone ringing at exactly 6:55p.m. every time that Billy Graham aired. My dear grandmother was calling to remind us that Billy Graham would be on at seven o'clock.

I waited several days for the airing of Billy Graham and when he appeared on my screen I was surprised to see that he looked so old and that he sounded even older than he looked. As I thought about it, what did I expect? I was fifty years old and I had been watching Billy Graham for as long as I could remember so of course he wouldn't be a young man!

Following the program I thought about the message and I thought about my grandmother. My grandmother is gone. Billy Graham is old and the message that he preaches is even older. It is the message of God loving the world so much that he sent his only Son to die for our sins so that we might have eternal life. It was a few days after watching Billy Graham that I got it.

There are facts and there are truths. (I know all about facts because my very most favorite daughter is in a doctoral program and she is always asking me about the facts of any event or situation. She is so smart. I was almost that smart when I was young. She frequently asks me the *basis* for my opinions and decicions.)

The fact is that life isn't fair. People hurt us and we hurt others. The truth is that we are not responsible for the actions of others, only our own. In taking responsibility for our own actions we can choose to be victims or we can choose to forgive and move forward.

Think about it. If God can forgive us our sins and if Sammy can forgive those who hurt and tried to hurt him, how can I not forgive? I get it!

Do I think that the sun will shine every day? No, I am fifty years old so I've been around long enough to know that there will be clouds and wind and rain. But I do know that while the sun doesn't always shine the Son always shines. I get it. Do you get it?

I accomplished my goal of survival and I have lived to tell about it. Since I seem to be goal oriented I have decided that a goal for middle age will be to lean forward in faith and grace and forgiveness.

May you have angels all around you and as a very special man always said in parting, "Till we meet again".

TRUTH: God loves you.